NEW DIRECTIONS FOR ADULT AND CONTINUING EDUCATION

Ralph G. Brockett, *University of Tennessee, Knoxville*
Susan Imel, *Ohio State University*
EDITORS-IN-CHIEF

Alan B. Knox, *University of Wisconsin, Madison*
CONSULTING EDITOR

W9-DCY-648

What Really Matters in Adult Education Program Planning: Lessons in Negotiating Power and Interests

Ronald M. Cervero
University of Georgia

Arthur L. Wilson
North Carolina State University

EDITORS

Number 69, Spring 1996

JOSSEY-BASS PUBLISHERS
San Francisco

WHAT REALLY MATTERS IN PROGRAM PLANNING:
LESSONS IN NEGOTIATING POWER AND INTERESTS
Ronald M. Cervero, Arthur L. Wilson (eds.)
New Directions for Adult and Continuing Education, no. 69
Ralph G. Brockett, Susan Imel, Editors-in-Chief
Alan B. Knox, Consulting Editor

ISSN 0195-2242   ISBN 0-7879-9866-4

NEW DIRECTIONS FOR ADULT AND CONTINUING EDUCATION is part of The
Jossey-Bass Higher and Adult Education Series and is published quarterly
by Jossey-Bass Inc., Publishers, 350 Sansome Street, San Francisco,
California 94104-1342. Second-class postage paid at San Francisco,
California, and at additional mailing offices. POSTMASTER: Send address
changes to New Directions for Adult and Continuing Education, Jossey-
Bass Inc., Publishers, 350 Sansome Street, San Francisco, California
94104-1342.

SUBSCRIPTIONS for 1996 cost $50.00 for individuals and $72.00 for institutions, agencies, and libraries.

EDITORIAL CORRESPONDENCE should be sent to the Editor-in-Chief,
Susan Imel, ERIC/ACVE, 1900 Kenny Road, Columbus, Ohio 43210-1090.
E-mail: imel.1@osu.edu.

Cover photograph by Wernher Krutein/PHOTOVAULT © 1990.

Manufactured in the United States of America on Lyons Falls
Pathfinder Tradebook. This paper is acid-free and 100 percent
totally chlorine-free.

CONTENTS

EDITORS' NOTES

In our book *Planning Responsibly for Adult Education: A Guide to Negotiating Power and Interests* (Cervero and Wilson, 1994), we described program planning as a social activity in which people negotiate personal and organizational interests. In our view, programs are planned by real people in complex organizations, both of which have their own traditions, political relationships, and needs and interests. All planners know that they are not free agents able to directly mold the purposes, content, and format of a program to satisfy their own interests. Rather, planning is always conducted within a complex set of personal, organizational, and social relationships among people who may have similar, different, or conflicting interests. Thus, program planners' responsibility—and the essential problem of their practice—centers on how to negotiate the interests of these people to construct a program.

Since our book was published, a number of practitioners and researchers have used the theoretical framework it described to examine program planning practice. In doing so, they have offered many useful insights for program planners regarding the political realities and ethical issues of everyday practice. We believe it is time to collect these insights and assess what we can learn from practice. The purpose of this sourcebook, then, is to identify the political and ethical issues faced by program planners in a variety of practice settings and the actual negotiation strategies they use in these settings. The case studies presented here reflect a variety of social and organizational contexts, ranging from university-based professional education to community-based education for social change.

In Chapter One we stress the importance of paying attention to the "people work" of planning and briefly review our understanding of planning practice as negotiating interests and power. Planning is defined as a social activity in which educators negotiate personal and organizational interests to construct educational programs for adults. Four central concepts are reviewed: power, interests, negotiation, and responsibility. Finally, we review the charge given to the authors of the six case study chapters that follow.

The case study by Barbara McDonald in Chapter Two examines a community-based planning effort initiated by a department of the federal government. The chapter asks whether community-based planning can be accomplished in the face of unequal power relationships. How can community activists effectively plan in the face of government power? McDonald describes purposeful action she has taken to equalize power relations between community activists and government planners and provides lessons for more democratic planning of community-based environmental education and environmental literacy programs.

The case study in Chapter Three involves another community-based planning context. In it, Teresa M. Carter examines the activities of a health promotion coalition that used an empowerment model to plan programs to reduce premature deaths due to AIDS and violence. Carter identifies ways in which the interests of the various planners affected the activities and outcomes stipulated by the empowerment model. She indicates that it is very likely that planning (in particular, empowerment planning) can get lost or subverted in the complex interplay of power relationships, interests, and structural and economic factors in the community. Thus, educators bent on empowering communities must work with the participants and direct their attention to strategies that will ensure that community interests are adequately represented at the planning table.

Susan M. Hendricks's case study in Chapter Four takes place in the ordinary, everyday world of a college nursing program. This case study examines the politics of planning in nursing education and offers strategies for bringing about change to better serve nursing students. Hendricks implores educational planners to look beneath the commonplaces of educational programming to see the dynamic, changing environment it inhabits, composed of power relationships, negotiated interests, and ethical issues. She shows that every communication that occurs among the members of the Nursing Achievement Program she describes and with various stakeholders influences future power relationships in the program. She argues that being aware of these dynamics is essential to good planning practice and that the planner who is aware of the effect of these everyday communications has the ability to achieve change and create programs that will develop in meaningful, desired directions.

In Chapter Five, Roger G. Maclean argues that program planners must realize that medical schools see continuing education as fulfilling many institutional needs, such as generating patient referrals to the university hospital. His chapter examines the political and ethical dilemmas faced by planners who must address multiple competing interests in developing continuing education programs. Maclean's main focus is on showing the political and ethical dilemmas faced by continuing educators when their programs are supposed to improve patient care, generate referrals to their university hospital, and make a profit for their institution.

In Chapter Six, Pamela B. Kleiber identifies the central issue faced by those who plan distance education in a university setting: the faculty's perception that this form of education is inferior. This perception can be a major impediment to the planning process, because all courses offered in a distance education format must be approved by the academic department. Kleiber demonstrates three negotiation strategies that she uses to level the playing field when working with faculty to develop curriculum for distance education programs: the use of technical data in the planning process, the use of a structured planning process, and formalized agreements with the academic departments.

The case study in Chapter Seven, by Sue M. Scott and Margo Schmitt-Boshnick, examines the collective planning of a community-based program for women. The chapter reviews the ethical issues that arose when the participatory planning practices of the women were contested by government funders, and it offers strategies for maintaining the integrity of collective planning processes. The authors' strategies for resolving their dilemmas included educating the government funders by including the women receiving services in the negotiation meetings.

Chapter Eight, by Thomas J. Sork, offers a critique of our planning theory and its application to the six case studies in this volume. He argues that although our work represents an important turning point in theorizing about program planning, much work needs to be done to extend the analysis and to understand its implications for program planning. In particular, he raises questions about the source of planners' power, the importance of planners' identities, and the quest for substantive democratic planning.

In the final chapter we suggest three recommendations for practice, drawing upon the six case studies and Sork's critique. First, we draw attention to the idea that planning requires a way of seeing and that responsible planning requires a particular way of seeing. Second, we suggest that learning to see is part of learning how to "read" planning situations. Finally, we synthesize several insights from the case studies about what really matters when planners see planning practice as a process of negotiating power and interests.

Ronald M. Cervero
Arthur L. Wilson
Editors

Reference

Cervero, R. M., and Wilson, A. L. *Planning Responsibly for Adult Education: A Guide to Negotiating Power and Interests.* San Francisco: Jossey-Bass, 1994.

RONALD M. CERVERO is professor in the Department of Adult Education, University of Georgia.

ARTHUR L. WILSON is assistant professor in the Department of Adult and Community College Education, North Carolina State University.

Experienced adult and continuing education program planners
know that they must pay attention to the "people work" of practice.
This chapter describes planning practice as a social activity in which
planners negotiate interests; it asks how planners manage the political
and ethical dimensions of their practice.

Paying Attention to the People Work When Planning Educational Programs for Adults

Arthur L. Wilson, Ronald M. Cervero

What do planners have to pay attention to when planning programs for adults? How do adult educators actually get their planning work done? Answers to these questions are central to understanding and improving program planning practice. Our view is that the program planning literature has neglected significant aspects of practice. Drawing on Schön's work (1983) on how professionals think and act in practice, we have reflected on our own planning experience and systematically investigated how adult and continuing education planners actually construct programs (Cervero and Wilson, 1994a). From that reflection and investigation, it is just as clear to us as to any experienced planner that planning practice requires far more than the technical skills stressed in the literature.

Theories do not plan programs—people do (Forester, 1989). Thus planning work always requires "people work": "Planners work on problems, with people. The problem work is potentially technical, but it may be more craft-like or routine; the people work is always political, sometimes explicitly so, at other times not" (p. 4). Experienced planners are constantly confronted with issues that involve people, such as what has to be done and what can be delayed, whose phone call to return and whose they can ignore, which problems need immediate attention, and who needs to be informed. Managing these complex social interactions are a crucial part of any planning process, requiring a set of skills not considered by the stepwise planning process promoted in the literature. For without political savvy and an ethical vision, without knowing who counts and why, without both a sense of "how to" and a vision of "what for," even faithful following of the prescribed planning process will have little consequence. What we often consider to be the "noise" of planning—telephone calls, faxes, meetings, the constant interruptions endemic to the modern organization—actually turns out to be the central theater of a planner's political activities. The current literature provides inadequate guidance for making the political and ethical decisions that are a constant component of this "people work" of planning.

To better understand the people work of planning, we have described planning as a social activity in which planners negotiate personal and organizational interests to construct educational programs for adults (Cervero and Wilson, 1994a, 1994b). In our view, real people plan programs in complex organizations, which have traditions, political relationships, and needs and interests that profoundly influence the planning process. In our previous work we showed that people's and organizational interests are causally related to which programs get constructed and which do not. In this chapter, we shift our attention to how planners actually negotiate interests—that is, which strategies they use in the varying contexts of their practice. The purpose of this sourcebook, then, is to identify the ethical and political issues that program planners face in a variety of practice settings and the actual negotiation strategies they use in planning programs. In this chapter we make an argument for the importance of the people work of planning and briefly review our understanding of planning practice as a process of negotiating interests and power.

People Plan Educational Programs

What are good planning practitioners supposed to do when planning educational programs for adults? Most textbooks advocate following the steps prescribed in program planning theory. Those steps, while varied in number and name, almost always include assessing needs, constructing objectives, selecting content, formulating methods, managing the program, and evaluating consequences. Sork and Buskey (1986) reviewed planning literature from 1950 to 1983 and found that these dimensions were consistently presented as essential in planning theory. In 1989 Sork and Caffarella arrived at virtually the same conclusion in depicting central planning tasks. Indeed, in our study of the historical evolution of adult education planning theory (Wilson and Cervero, 1995), we saw that earlier versions of these basic procedural tasks first emerged in the 1930s and became so well established by the 1950s that they have been accepted without question ever since. The procedural principles are certainly important—in fact, good planning depends substantially upon the technical ability of adult educators to design needs assessments, formulate objectives, select content, manage programs, and evaluate results. But there are two related problems with these prescriptions that dominate the literature.

First, the literature only addresses the more technical aspects of planning practice. Experienced planners, however, routinely report that they have had to learn many lessons that are not accounted for in these planning models, such as how to decide who should be involved in the needs assessment, how to capitalize on opportunities or avoid hazards, how to compete for scarce resources, and how to convince colleagues and superiors of the value of their programs. This is no surprise, for Schön's investigations (1983) show that as professionals become more experienced they increasingly rely on their own past actions to build a repertoire of practice knowledge and skill that enables them to work more effectively than textbook knowledge would allow. As in the planning disciplines in general (Forester, 1989), adult and continuing educators must go beyond the technical principles and rely on their more deeply situated knowledge of how to actually plan programs. There is a growing research tradition in adult and continuing education that addresses the need for an understanding of program planning beyond the stepwise models presented in the past (Brookfield, 1986; Casey, 1989; Mills, Cervero, Langone, and Wilson, 1995; Pennington and Green, 1976; Wissemann, 1991). Sandmann (1993) makes the point directly in her study of cooperative extension agents: "The educators didn't see program development as a step-by-step process. . . . They spent much of their time trying to alleviate the tensions that resulted from conflicts between the amount of time available, and inevitable interruptions among differing organizational clientele, community, and personal goals" (p. 20). So the first problem with the literature is that at best it focuses on the more technical aspects of planning practice. In so doing, it misses discussing the people work, which "alleviates the tensions," as Sandmann says.

The second problem with the literature emerges from the first. The reason planners do not—indeed, often cannot—follow the steps prescribed by program planning theory is that the organizational power relationships within which they must act always profoundly structure their planning actions. Traditional planning theory tells practitioners to simply follow the steps, as if the constraints and opportunities of the social and organizational context do not matter. The problem with this prescription is that program planning always occurs in organizations in which planners' actions are shaped by resource competition and limitations, shifting alliances and demands, institutional policies, and power relations. While planning theory often recognizes that the context may require planners to deal with technical demands situationally— that is, out of sequence (for example, see Houle, 1972; Sork and Caffarella, 1989)—it rarely provides any guidance for practitioners who must act within their specific organizational context (Giddens, 1979). Sork and Caffarella (1989) best capture the issue when they report that adult and continuing educators "usually understand how contextual factors influence their work" (p. 235), which they describe as organizational history, mission statements, resource availability, competitive environments, and community relations. While they point to the right sorts of contextual factors, they exemplify most planning theory by remaining vague on just what it is that planners "usually understand" about their settings and how to act in them. This complex interplay of people acting within structured organizational and social power relationships to get things done, while alluded to, is rarely a central source of insight in the planning literature. Issues worth understanding include knowing the organizational ropes and not just the organizational chart, managing communication among sometimes cooperating and sometimes competing colleagues and superiors, securing scarce resources, hedging bets and taking long shots, and knowing when to move quickly to seize opportunities and when to retrench quietly to cover losses. In sum, planning involves much people work, and this people work is shaped profoundly by structured power relationships within work settings. Programs emerge from the everyday judgments planners make while carrying out this people work. Yet, people work is not a primary source of insights about planning in the traditional models.

Because planning theories in general do not offer an understanding of politically structured people work, which requires judgments about what to do in specific settings, they are able to offer very little guidance on how planners must act. In our view, what is practical for planners to do varies across organizational situations, political climates, and ethical beliefs. What is missing from most planning theory is how planning is always an integration of individual planners' actions and the organizational context in which they work. What is possible depends more on what is doable within the political structure of that context rather than on what is achievable according to traditional planning procedure. What planners must understand is how to use their organizational know-how, based on their practical experience of getting things done, to craft "a history of working conversations that link interested parties" (Forester, 1989, p. 10), conversations and alliances that allow planners to take full advantage of their technical problem-solving skills. Until we have a better understanding of how planners routinely act in the structured social interaction of complex organizations, traditional planning theory's major value lies in naming the technical tasks of planning.

People Work Is Always Political

The two related problems we have just sketched—needing to understand the people work that planners do and to understand how they go about doing it—lead directly to the major concern of this sourcebook. We believe that whenever adult and continuing educators plan programs, they engage in a social activity consisting of negotiating personal and organizational interests. Furthermore, the social and organizational contexts in which they plan are characterized by historically developing and structurally organized relations of power. Because people must regularly make judgments to construct educational programs in the messy world of organizations, planning theory must address two central issues. First, as we have seen, whenever people act in a social context, they do so within structured power relationships. Every experienced planner knows that the politics of the situation always matters, regardless of whether consensus or conflict marks the political relationships. Second, if people always plan in the face of power (Forester, 1989), to whom are they responsible for the educational programs they construct? Any account of program planning must address both power and responsibility in order to be of any practical help in the everyday world.

In our earlier work, we developed four central concepts that can account for the world that planners experience: power, interests, negotiation, and responsibility. These four concepts show us what to pay attention to in planning practice. We argue that planners' work is always carried out in contexts that are marked by power relationships that will enable or constrain responsible planning. Because people's interests are causally related to the kinds of educational programs that are constructed, negotiation is the characteristic activity of program planning practice. The central responsibility of planners' practice, then, is to work out whose interests will be represented in the planning process. This characteristic planning activity—negotiating interests within organizational power relationships—always has two outcomes: planners "construct" educational programs, and through their practices, they "reconstruct," either maintaining or transforming, the power relationships and interests that make planning possible.

Power Relationships Frame Planning Contexts

Our starting point is that planning practice, like any other human activity, is located within a social dynamic. As we have seen, planning nearly always involves working with other people, so we have to think about it in terms of the "enduring social relationships" (Isaac, 1987, p. 51) that support or constrain planners' working relations and planning actions. The fundamental enduring social relationship that structures the context in which planners routinely work is power: who has it and what they do with it. Giddens (1979) argues that power, which is the socially structured capacity to act and not just a personal attribute, is a central feature of these relationships: "action only exists when an agent has the capability of intervening, or refraining from intervening, in a series of events so as to be able to influence their course" (p. 256). While action is the result of human intention, the ability to act is structurally distributed. In this view, power is the capacity to act, distributed to individual planners by virtue of their organizational and social position (Isaac, 1987). Such an understanding recasts the traditional position of the planner as a disinterested technical expert who provides information to solve problems. While even seasoned planners routinely decry their lack of power, what they really mean is that they typically have less power than others whose interests direct program construction. So planners have power to act by virtue of their organizational position, and their constant political problem is how to use it to construct their programs.

Interests Produce Programs

Interests, which direct the actions of all people in the planning process, are complex sets of "predispositions, embracing goals, values, desires, expectations, and other orientations and expectations that lead a person to act in one direction or another" (Morgan, 1986, p. 41). Interests, then, are the motivations and purposes that lead people to act in certain ways when confronted with situations in which they must make a judgment about what to do or say. Quite simply, people's interests directly produce programs. In the traditional models, planners are supposed to use their technical information and skills to discover program purposes and outcomes. We believe that, more fundamentally, educational programs are causally related to the exercise of power in relation to people's interests, which always matter in determining program purposes, content, and formats. That education programs are causally related to people's interests is not an insignificant point. We must ask, "If programs do not depend on people's interests, upon what do they depend?" or, perhaps more importantly, "If programs are not causally related to people's interests, why does it matter which educational programs are constructed?" Programs do not emerge, then, from the technical application of planning principles but rather from the intersection of planners' and others' interests. In sum, power relationships structure the terrain on which people must act, and their interests provide their motivations for acting on that terrain.

Program Planning Is Negotiation

In order to make the direct connection between the acting planner and the organizational context, we argue that negotiation is the central form of action that planners undertake. Programs result, then, not from the application of planning principles but from the negotiation of multiple interests and power relationships. Planners always negotiate in two dimensions simultaneously. First, and most obviously, their actions construct an educational program. For this we draw upon the conventional usage of *negotiation*, which is defined in the 1976 *Webster's New World Dictionary* as "to confer, bargain, or discuss with a view to reaching agreement." Within this conventional usage, planners not only bring their own interests to the planning process (*negotiate with*) but must constantly *negotiate between* others' interests to construct a program. Second, and at a more fundamental and encompassing level, planners also *negotiate about* the interests and power relationships themselves. People's interests and power relationships are not static but are continually being acted upon by the negotiation process itself. Planners' actions, while they are directed toward constructing educational programs, are also always reconstructing the power relationships and interests of everyone involved in the planning process (and of people who are not involved as well). We argue that power relationships and interests always both structure planners' actions (negotiation) and are reconstructed by them. In other words, planners act both within and upon their context. As planners act, they can expect to construct a visible program that will affect the world in a certain way; they will also reconstruct, less visibly, the power relationships and interests involved in terms of "knowledge (who knows what), consent (who exercises power and who obeys), trust (who cooperates with whom), and the formulation of problems (who focuses on or neglects which problems)" (Forester, 1989, p. 80).

Planners Must Negotiate Interests Responsibly

All planners know that they are not free agents able to translate their interests directly into the purposes, content, and format of programs. Rather, their planning is always conducted within a complex set of personal and organizational power relationships among people who may have similar, different, or conflicting interests regarding the program. Therefore, planners' responsibility, and the central problem of their practice, centers on how to negotiate among the interests of these people to construct a program. Drawing on the 1976 *Webster's New World Dictionary* again, we take *responsibility* as being able "to answer for one's conduct or obligation, [to be] politically answerable." The practical problem is to answer this question in every concrete planning activity: to whom is the adult and continuing educator ethically and politically answerable? If the actual form and content of programs depend on the interests of those who construct them, then the central ethical question becomes "Whose interests will planners represent?" and the central political question becomes "How will planners negotiate those interests?"

In our view, all planning practice takes an ethical stance about whose interests matter and then relies on political skills to negotiate those interests. To answer these ethical questions in practice requires a specific vision or belief system. For if a planning theory is to inform the judgments planners routinely make in negotiating interests, it must be rooted in an ethic that is not based solely on power. Our theory of planning practice rests on the belief that adult and continuing educators should actively promote a substantively democratic planning process. Because interests are constantly negotiated in planning, our vision of democratic planning means that all people who are affected by a program should "be involved in the deliberation of what is important" (Apple, 1992, p. 11). Thus, nurturing a substantively democratic planning process means, simply, putting real choices before people about what collective action to take in constructing a program. Thus, planners must ask themselves in every situation, "In what ways are my actions promoting substantive involvement?" This belief makes our planning theory instructive for practice by providing an ethical basis for practical judgments about what to do in specific situations. In a very real sense, this interest in democratizing planning is our vision of how educational programs should be constructed. As Apple (1990) points out, "Democracy is not a slogan to be called upon when the 'real business' of our society is over, but a constitutive principle that must be integrated into all of our daily lives" (p. xvi). In our view, being politically answerable—that is, responsible—as planners requires an active alignment of substantive democratic action with our political skills for negotiating interests and power.

Although planners' strategic vision should be that all people who are affected by a program have the right to participate in constructing it, knowing which people should be involved and how to create conditions for their substantive involvement is almost always an uncertain, ambiguous, and risky activity. No theory can unambiguously determine whether the actual people selected to construct a program are, in some transcendental sense, the right people. Rather, the planner must make a practical judgment in each and every situation. In light of this, we suggest a scheme for recognizing whose interests are at stake in any educational program. Expanding on the work of others (for example, Knox, 1982), we believe that there are five groups of people whose interests always matter in planning programs: learners, teachers, planners, institutional leaders, and the affected public. The interests of these five groups are always negotiated in some way. The crucial practical issues are who actually represents their interests, whether they are legitimate representatives, and whether they are the best representatives available given the specific circumstances.

Understanding Practice: What Do We Need to Know?

We have two reasons for beginning this sourcebook with our understanding of planning as a social process of negotiating power and interests. The first is to explain what we know at this point about planning practice. We know that interests are causally related to which programs are constructed and that power matters in terms of whose interests are represented. Initially we reported on three extensive case studies that showed clearly that the personal and organizational interests represented by the planner directly affect the purposes, content, and format of programs (Cervero and Wilson, 1994a). In paying attention to the people work—as Forester says, the crafting of working conversations that link interested parties—planners characteristically negotiate interests in organizational contexts in which power relationships structure their ability to act.

Our second reason is to provide evidence and explanation as background for the chapters that follow. Based on what we know, we can begin asking new questions. Since we have some sense of what matters (power and interests) and what planners do (negotiate), we now shift the question to how planners actually negotiate power and interests. That is, which negotiation strategies do they actually use in managing the people work of their planning practice, and what are the ethical frameworks that guide their choices and justify their planning actions? In this sense, we are moving from the question of what planners do to how they do it. That is the charge we have placed upon each of the following authors. All are experienced planners who reflect upon how they and other people negotiate power and interests in specific programmatic and institutional contexts. Their reports and analysis rely directly on the views we have expressed here, in hopes of moving forward our understanding of what planners "usually understand" (Sork and Caffarella, 1989, p. 235) about how to act in their planning contexts to get things done.

References

Apple, M. W. *Ideology and Curriculum.* (2nd ed.) New York: Routledge & Kegan Paul, 1990.

Apple, M. W. "The Text and Cultural Politics." *Educational Researcher,* 1992, *21* (7), 4–11, 19.

Brookfield, S. D. *Understanding and Facilitating Adult Learning: A Comprehensive Analysis of Principles and Effective Practices.* San Francisco: Jossey-Bass, 1986.

Casey, M. A. "Program Planning Processes Used by Minnesota Extension Service Agriculture Agents." *Dissertation Abstracts International,* 1989, *50,* 2748A.

Cervero, R. M., and Wilson, A. L. *Planning Responsibly for Adult Education: A Guide to Negotiating Power and Interests.* San Francisco: Jossey-Bass, 1994a.

Cervero, R. M., and Wilson, A. L. "The Politics of Responsibility: A Theory of Program Planning Practice for Adult Education." *Adult Education Quarterly,* 1994b, *45* (1), 249–268.

Forester, J. *Planning in the Face of Power.* Berkeley: University of California Press, 1989.

Giddens, A. *Central Problems in Social Theory: Action, Structure, and Contradiction in Social Analysis.* Berkeley: University of California Press, 1979.

Houle, C. O. *The Design of Education.* San Francisco: Jossey-Bass, 1972.

Isaac, J. C. *Power and Marxist Theory: A Realist View.* Ithaca, N.Y.: Cornell University Press, 1987.

Knox, A. B. (ed.). *Leadership Strategies for Meeting New Challenges.* New Directions for Continuing Education, no. 13. San Francisco: Jossey-Bass, 1982.

Mills, D. P., Cervero, R. M., Langone, C. A., and Wilson, A. L. "The Impact of Interests, Power Relationships, and Organizational Structure on Program Planning Practice: A Case Study." *Adult Education Quarterly,* 1995, *46* (1), 1–16.

Morgan, G. *Images of Organization.* Thousand Oaks, Calif.: Sage, 1986.

Pennington, F., and Green, J. "Comparative Analysis of Program Development in Six Professions." *Adult Education,* 1976, *27,* 13–23.

Sandmann, L. R. "Why Programs Aren't Implemented as Planned." *Journal of Extension,* Winter 1993, *31,* 18–21.

Schön, D. A. *The Reflective Practitioner.* New York: Basic Books, 1983.

Sork, T. J., and Buskey, J. H. "A Descriptive and Evaluative Analysis of Program Planning Literature, 1950–1983." *Adult Education Quarterly,* 1986, *36,* 86–96.

Sork, T. J., and Caffarella, R. S. "Planning Programs for Adults." In S. B. Merriam and P. M. Cunningham (eds.), *Handbook of Adult and Continuing Education.* San Francisco: Jossey-Bass, 1989.

Wilson, A. L., and Cervero, R. M. "Siting Program Planning Theory in Adult Education: The Selective Tradition of Privileging Technical Rationality." In *Proceedings of the 36th Annual Adult Education Research Conference.* Edmonton, Canada: University of Alberta, 1995.

Wissemann, A. F. "Processes Used by Selected Illinois Extension Agents (Advisors) to Provide High Quality Programs." Unpublished doctoral dissertation, University of Illinois, Urbana-Champaign, 1991.

ARTHUR L. WILSON is assistant professor in the Department of Adult and Community College Education, North Carolina State University.

RONALD M. CERVERO is professor in the Department of Adult Education, University of Georgia.

*Low-income and minority communities are often denied opportunities
to help design environmental education programs relevant to their
environmental experience and needs. As the weaker partner in
government-initiated programs, community activists often struggle
to find their voice in the planning process.*

Counteracting Power Relationships When Planning Environmental Education

Barbara McDonald

The right to have knowledge about one's physical environment has recently
emerged as an issue in communities of color and those characterized by low
incomes and other social, economic, and political disadvantages. These communities have been shown to bear a disproportionate share of the nation's environmental pollution. In 1987, the United Church of Christ's Commission for
Racial Justice released findings on the demographics of populations living near
toxic waste sites (cited in Sexton, Olden, and Johnson, 1993). The commission
reported that communities with one or more commercial hazardous-waste facilities also had a significantly higher proportion of racial minorities than communities without such facilities. Similar studies published in the 1990s, as well
as conferences, summits, and meetings on what is now known as environmental justice, continue to highlight the severity of the problem and to galvanize
action to address the issue. In 1992 the Environmental Protection Agency published a report recommending the involvement of racial minorities and low-
income communities in environmental policy making (cited in Sexton, Olden,
and Johnson, 1993). In 1993 President Clinton issued Executive Order No.
12898, which directed all federal agencies to address environmental justice in
low-income and minority communities (Bullard, 1994). Although some
researchers prefer the term *environmental racism* to highlight the disparity
between the environmental risks borne by predominantly nonwhite communities compared to predominantly white communities, most have adopted the
term *environmental justice* to focus attention on the need for all citizens to attain
environmental equity (Sexton, Olden, and Johnson, 1993). One strategy that

may be employed to facilitate community knowledge and empowerment in issues of environmental justice is environmental education.

Environmental education and environmental literacy are disproportionately low in the very communities that bear higher environmental risks. Environmental knowledge is more prevalent in better educated, more affluent communities. In addition, environmental information and curricula are typically developed by white, middle-class science educators. Information developed from the white middle-class perspective usually does not consider the specific environmental settings, experiences, problems, and issues faced by low-income and minority communities. Wals (1994) notes that in addition to being the target of inappropriate or irrelevant environmental education programs, low-income and minority communities are often the victims of irresponsible and disempowering environmental and social inquiry. He stresses the need for "methods of inquiry . . . which will allow those who are affected by education and educational change to express their ideas, to point out inequalities in resource access and power imbalances and to help determine changes that they themselves find important" (p. 15). Further, Wals claims that environmental education should be redefined as "the process that enables students and [educators] to participate more fully in the planning, implementing, and evaluating of educational activities aimed at resolving an environmental issue that the learners have identified" (p. 18).

Environmental education is the responsibility of various federal agencies. This chapter reports on a program-planning process initiated by a department of the federal government. The names of the department, the project, and the participants have been changed to maintain anonymity.

The U.S. Agriculture Agency views environmental education as a minor but critical tool for informing and enhancing its long-term agricultural management goals. Typically more involved in rural communities, the Agriculture Agency entered the urban arena with the development of the CityGreen Project, a community-based environmental education program. Initially developed in a large southern city, the CityGreen Project expanded to become a network of cooperative environmental education programs across the country, with participants usually centered on neighborhood parks. CityGreen educational activities are organized and conducted with a wide variety of partners, and local knowledge is incorporated into all aspects of the program. Thus, planning CityGreen projects is usually a complex affair with strong local input and involvement. Because CityGreen projects are locally developed, each project is a little different.

The Agriculture Agency is no stranger to planning models that include community involvement. By law the agency must involve the public in all agricultural planning. Community-based planning for urban environmental education, in the form of the CityGreen Project, was a logical extension of the Agriculture Agency's rural activities, and it was an appropriate response to Executive Order No. 12898. In a review of the first ten years of public involvement in planning for Agriculture Agency projects, a federal report noted that the planning process should educate everyone involved: "education is one of the most important results and functions of planning" (Larsen and others, 1990, p. 2). In addition, the report emphasized that *"planning is not the exclusive domain of experts, planners, and technical processes. . . .* Planning must address issues about which people deeply care. . . . Planning is immersed in our country's social and political milieu" (p. 3, italics in original).

Nevertheless, community-based planning is not simple or easily accomplished. The responsible planner must be aware of the power relationships and interests influencing the planning activity (Cervero and Wilson, 1994). These can be especially troublesome factors in community-based planning initiated by the government. In such initiatives, power is typically unequally distributed among planning participants, with the community being the weaker partner (McArthur, 1993). In many cases, moreover, government planners may use their stronger position to advocate actions that they say represent the best interests of the community, even when there is evidence to the contrary. Thus, government-sponsored community-based initiatives are marked by unequal power and influence, with government interests often overriding community interests and concerns.

The rest of this chapter describes the planning of a specific CityGreen project. The planning was coordinated by an Agriculture Agency planner, but representatives from all levels of government and from the private sector were involved. This case study considers whether community-based planning for environmental education can be accomplished in a setting characterized by unequal power relationships. It describes purposeful actions that can be taken to equalize participants' power and provides lessons for a more democratic planning process for community-based environmental education and environmental literacy programs.

Program Context and Description

The CityGreen Project was established in the early 1990s in a large southern city. Due to the program's success and popularity, the Agriculture Agency decided to employ a full-time planner to support efforts to develop CityGreen projects in other communities. The planner's responsibilities are to develop procedures and standards and to provide promotional materials and direct assistance to interested communities. I am that planner, and I was also the developer of the original CityGreen Project concept. I have both a real and an expressed interest in promoting the concept of collaborative planning and in involving communities in planning environmental education and environmental literacy programs. (As described by Cervero and Wilson [1994], a person's real interests are a product of his or her implicit values and norms. Expressed interests are those that an individual claims overtly.)

I became involved in the Maryville CityGreen project after I was directed to work there by the chief officer in my section of the Agriculture Agency. Maryville is a medium-sized city in the southern United States. Maynard State

University, located in Maryville, is a predominantly black university with strong ties to the Agriculture Agency. Its agricultural program has received numerous large Agriculture Agency grants and awards, and therefore the Agriculture Agency has an investment in Maynard University's continued success.

Maynard's dean of agriculture is a large, imposing individual who is accustomed to getting his way. He is a charming middle-aged African American. He is well educated, determined, successful, and a visionary. He also has a reputation for being dominating and vengeful, and rarely, if ever, has he been challenged by his faculty, his colleagues, or the community. He and his faculty have developed a limited number of partnerships with representatives from state and local government and with a few nonprofit groups, but by and large Maynard's community outreach has been paltry.

As Maynard must compete with other state educational institutions for increasingly scarce government funds, the dean had a vision of developing a highly visible, statewide agricultural center that would include hands-on education. The CityGreen Project presented an opportunity for Maynard to gain statewide and national attention for an innovative program and to attract support from governments, business and industry, and nonprofit organizations across the state. These motivations represented the dean's real interests: he was interested in building a program that would bring renown both to his academic career and his institution's image. His expressed interests included providing opportunities for environmental education to individuals throughout the state, without regard to their race or income, and ensuring that the program would not be seen as focusing only on minority populations.

However, this statewide vision for the Maryville CityGreen project was in direct opposition to the vision that I, as developer and planner, had for the project. In some measure it was also at odds with the Agriculture Agency's vision of local community involvement and planning, as well as its environmental justice goals. A project directed toward statewide participation would likely fail to reflect the environmental experiences and educational needs of low-income and minority communities. It would tend to reproduce the type of generalized curricula typical of mainstream environmental education.

When I first arrived at Maynard, I was unaware of the dean's statewide vision. As project planning progressed, it became clear that the dean was determined to have the project developed his way, regardless of others' positions or preferences. My goal as planner shifted from the obvious one of planning the project to a more covert goal of counteracting and diffusing the dean's power. I felt a responsibility to try to equalize the power relationships at play in the planning process to enable community representatives to have a voice. But counteracting power can be professionally dangerous in a highly charged, political situation. Therefore, my primary strategy became one of nurturing other significant players, those who also had some measure of power and who shared my vision of a community-based project. I hoped that these individuals would counteract the dean's power in ways I could not. At the first meeting, which also involved Maynard's local and state government partners and a few nonprofit representatives, I presented my vision of a collaborative, community-based environmental education project. The idea was embraced by a number of the attendees, including a nonprofit organization president, Amanda McKee. She became my major planning ally.

McKee is a longtime supporter of Maynard's agricultural program. A wealthy and philanthropic white woman, she has endowed academic scholarships at Maynard and contributed countless hours to promoting the agricultural program. Propelled by her personal convictions, she established an advocacy organization for urban beautification; in the process she discovered that she is well organized, intelligent, persuasive, and capable of achieving great success. Like others, she had never challenged Maynard's dean of agriculture but instead had chosen to work "with" the dean to achieve common goals. Her enthusiasm for the CityGreen Project concept, as I presented it, was unbounded. She immediately flew to the site of the original CityGreen project to see it in operation and to talk to local residents. She returned to Maryville even more committed to the community-based version of the project. A number of other local government and community partners in Maryville also adopted the community-based vision.

There were three other important players in this project. One of the local government partners, Ray Green, is an agricultural professional in the mayor's office. He understood the political necessity of supporting Maynard's position (which was, basically, the dean's), but he believed that a community-based CityGreen project in Maryville would be more successful and effective. A well-respected professional, his involvement is viewed as critical to the success of any such project, regardless of how it is configured. He is intelligent and levelheaded, but his greatest advantage is his political savvy. Green anticipates issues and problems and seeks solutions in advance. At the very least, he "covers all the bases" so that any contingencies are anticipated and addressed.

Sean Wilson, a state agricultural professional, was also a key player in the planning of the Maryville CityGreen project. Wilson saw the advantages in both approaches. He decided to support the statewide concept because his agency could then use the Maryville site to deliver its environmental education programs. Wilson is a quiet man, but in the words of McKee, "If he wants a statewide CityGreen Project, Wilson will work until he gets one." Robert Adamson is on Maynard's agricultural faculty. Out of approximately eight faculty members, he is the only one who "gets out into the community," according to McKee. He seems to do everything, and everything seems to fall on his shoulders. He reports that his actions are carefully monitored by the dean, and he is therefore very careful about what he says and does. Consequently, he did not feel at liberty to express his opinion about the CityGreen Project.

Over approximately eighteen months, I met with various combinations of the above group (along with other, less key individuals). Once the dean's power, influence, and desire for a statewide project became clear, I initiated a number of actions to influence the planning process so that a community-based project might have a chance to emerge. These included both formal and informal written and verbal communications, data collection, and site visits. At times I simply failed to take action. For example, I suggested to the dean that he find local residents who might support the statewide project. In response, he told me about a woman he knows who lives close to the Maryville site. Although he said nothing, it was clear he expected me to make the contact. Rather than pursue the contact, however, I did nothing. As a consequence, most of the planning meetings were void of any residents who live close to the chosen project site. The Maryville CityGreen project planning effort is, as of this writing, still under way. What has emerged so far from the planning process is a story of opposing personal and political wills and ideologies. As individuals have interacted and communicated with one another, some have gained strength and found their voice. The planning process has unfolded as a surprising and daring challenge to the established power and influence of the dean.

Negotiation, Politics, and Ethics

As a planner, I used a number of strategies to influence the planning process. The CityGreen Project is touted as a community-driven program. Therefore, I refrain from being directive, although I attempt to exert an influence based on my "expert" position as the program's national coordinator. One of my underlying strategies is to present myself as the planning expert. I have done this more frequently in Maryville than in other cities planning CityGreen projects, because in other cities the basic issue typically has not been whether the project will be community-driven or government-driven (a statewide project would almost certainly be government-driven). When the situation calls for it, I use my "expert" knowledge to caution community members about the dangers of straying too far from the established, tried-and-true CityGreen Project model. In other situations I emphasize the importance of each community's designing its CityGreen project in the manner that best meets its needs, whether it follows the established model or not.

At a basic level, I use my expert position as the basis for giving professional "advice," while actually advancing my real interests, which are to promote the establishment of community-driven environmental education programs. My expressed interests vary according to how I can best satisfy these real interests. I am a temporary government employee, and in the current political climate the chances of my keeping my job get smaller every day. Thus, keeping my job becomes less important as it becomes less likely. In the past I worried about the dean's reaction to my planning strategies. Now, however, I am much less intimidated by the dean's intimated threat to contact my supervisors if I do not support his position. As keeping my job has become less important, I have gained more power, or a greater capacity to act in accordance with my real interests.

A pivotal question remains regarding the dean's approach to the CityGreen Project planning process: why did the dean, who is accustomed to wielding his power by decree, not directly exert his influence in this case? I am a white, middle-aged, well-educated professional woman, and I operate with confidence in planning meetings. The dean has never figured out how much power and influence I really have, as a representative of the Agriculture Agency. He knows I have access to upper-level administrators and that I have their support. The Agriculture Agency is a major source of funding for Maynard; therefore, he cannot run the risk of alienating the agency. He has tried to subtly influence me, to persuade me to support his vision. He has not yet figured out that my approval or support is not necessary. McKee told me that the dean believes I am a key authority figure, and because of this belief, he will only push his views so far. In order to take advantage of my capacity to act (my power), I have encouraged this misconception.

For example, the meeting in which we were to vote on the Maryville City-Green project location was critical to the project's direction. The dean stacked the deck by bringing eleven faculty members and students to the meeting; those supporting a community-based project were easily outnumbered. Cries of protest were quickly silenced by the dean, who said, "We agreed that whoever was here would vote." The following day, I called him and told him I could not live with what happened. We would have to take another vote, and Maynard University could have only two representatives. He was angry, but he agreed. My intent was to put direct pressure on him. I hoped to salvage the community-based project by enabling previously silenced voices to have their say. I quickly discovered the damage was irreparable, however. Rather than going quietly away, the group that supported a community-based project had already met separately and made a most incredible decision: they would build their own CityGreen project, separate from the Maynard project. In doing so they directly challenged the dean's power and influence.

How had this group, which had previously been fearful of challenging the dean, gathered the courage to take such a step? Although they undoubtedly had many conversations among themselves, my actions as a planner encouraged and supported the development and expression of their collective voice. As a planner, I was biased in favor of a community-based CityGreen project in Maryville. This, I believe, was evident in my actions, even though I tried to cloak them in impartiality when working with representatives from Maynard. On the other hand, I openly encouraged those who supported a community-based project not to give up and to feel empowered to disagree with the dean. I was not fully successful in this goal with the original group. I tried a number of strategies to empower previously silenced voices during the first phase of the planning process. My intent was to use community voices to persuade the dean to adopt a community-based project. Community residents, however, were unwilling to challenge the dean's position.

One of my strategies was to research the different planners' views. I did this to achieve two objectives. First, by confidentially interviewing each of the seventeen individuals involved, not only would I gain an understanding of where everyone stood on the issue, but also the exercise would hopefully help them find their voice. Second, I would present the results of the interviews to empower those who disagreed with the dean to speak up—to let them see that they were not alone in their views. Of the seventeen individuals I interviewed, several were residents from the local community. During the interviews, they spoke freely of their interest and willingness to work on a local environmental education project. I reasoned that by speaking for them through an impartial research presentation, they would feel less intimidated to speak up for themselves in meetings. In regard to the local residents, I was wrong. Although I believe they wanted to disagree with the dean, they remained silent.

Thus my research strategy was only partially successful. It was successful insofar as McKee, after hearing the results, felt more sure than ever that a community-based CityGreen project was the right choice for Maryville. Outside the meetings, she began talking with others whom she knew felt the same. And when the dean stacked the vote at the meeting referred to above, McKee finally protested. She left in anger, but not before she expressed her feelings to the dean. This, to my knowledge, was one of the first times anyone had directly challenged him. When I suggested to him that he probably did not want to alienate McKee, a strong financial supporter of his program, he said, "Oh, she'll get over it." My gentle nudging of the dean toward compromise, although not successful, was another strategy that only hinted at a threat: "If you anger McKee, you will lose her as a supporter, and I don't think you can afford to do that." The dean remained convinced that everything would go his way.

The next day, the group that had decided to pursue a separate, community-based project began planning its effort. McKee asked me to come to their first planning meeting, and I went. The following week, I attended a planning meeting at Maynard; it was attended by only a few partners. Wilson, who had volunteered to chair the Maynard committee, was not present. At one of the earlier meetings, I had insisted (in my "expert" capacity) that it was not wise for Maynard University to take the lead in planning the Maryville CityGreen project. I said that the leadership needed to be shared. I used this strategy to accomplish two things: to lighten the work load on Robert Adamson, the Maynard faculty member who inherited all the work and who was far too busy to give the project the attention it needed, and to pull some of the power over the project away from the dean. I felt that the dean would try to control every detail, to the detriment of the project. I wanted to preserve whatever potential for collaboration and community input still existed. Although the dean could have overruled me, he accepted my expert advice. But, to my dismay, Wilson was not present at the Maynard meeting. Only two non-Maynard attendees were at the table. The dean confronted me, angry that I had attended the community-based group's planning meeting. He wondered how my supervisors would feel about this. How could I justify attending that meeting? He threatened to "do anything needed" to stop the community-based CityGreen project. I suggested that rather than retaliate, the dean should call a meeting with the other group to discuss the issue. I wanted to avoid an ugly scene, and the dean's tone was menacing. Since everyone else in the room agreed with this strategy, the dean hesitantly gave his approval and delegated the task to an attendee in the room.

After leaving the meeting, I called McKee and told her the dean was angry about their intention to move forward with a separate effort. I knew McKee would take immediate action. She scheduled an appointment with the dean for the following day, to "get this thing settled." She was gentle but firm as she explained how the two Maryville CityGreen projects could work together. McKee, in effect, was being the planner I could not be. In McKee, and to a lesser extent in others, I nurtured trust and self-confidence, until they felt comfortable challenging the dean and insisting on a more democratic, community-driven process. I could not challenge him directly myself, since I had adopted a nonpartisan stance from the beginning. In addition, a direct challenge would not have been supported by my agency and therefore would have failed for political reasons. In reality, I am not nonpartisan, and I care about what is happening in Maryville. I believe the community needs to be included in the planning, and I have tried a number of direct and indirect strategies to ensure its involvement and voice.

Planning a CityGreen project involves a series of political actions. The various players' interests guide how they act and react to the settings and relationships that evolve throughout the process. The politics of planning becomes much more complex, and diverse interests can undermine efforts to create a substantively democratic planning process. In the case of the Maryville project, the political issues included personal and organizational power, control, reputation, and acclaim. The question of democracy was never raised. The most essential part of the planning process, from my perspective as a planner, was to seeking strategies to reduce the power of the dean and increase the power of the community representatives. I needed someone to ask the democracy question for me. My main strategy, the one around which all my other strategies revolved, was to develop a relationship with the one individual I felt could successfully challenge the dean's power. But I had to nurture that relationship and encourage that individual to take action.

In the case of McKee, this was easy to do. A loving, kind, and generous woman, McKee and I quickly became friends. Our discussions were commonly characterized by exchanging information, comparing notes, and developing ideas. She invited me to stay at her house. We had dinner together, and we talked frequently. McKee's personal and professional development was promoted by a prestigious appointment to a national committee and by her being awarded a sizable grant to promote her beautification work. She began to see the dean in a different light. Her professional success helped her gain courage and openly disagree with him. On the other hand, McKee is not interested in making enemies. She is politically savvy, and she knows that cooperation is the key to success. Thus, she was the perfect individual to negotiate with the dean in my place.

The ethics of this situation are complex. As a planner, I had to remain true to my real interests, that is, my commitment to a collaborative and cooperative environmental education planning process. In so doing, however, I provided unequal amounts of information to different players (withholding information from the dean, for example, and providing it to McKee). Some in the Agriculture Agency thought that keeping the dean happy was of paramount importance. Thus, by some accounts, my actions brought into question my responsibility and loyalty to the agency. I encouraged disruption of relationships that had been stable. The damage to some of those relationships will never be fully repaired. As an outcome of this planning effort, the city is facing the development of two programs, which may strain the already scarce resources of Maryville.

On the other hand, my planning efforts have had at least a small positive impact on a budding professional's development. And the dean, even if he does not recognize it now, will benefit in the long run from facing this challenge to his power and influence. As government dollars become more scarce, he will need to adopt a more accommodating, cooperative, and partnering attitude. Therefore, the hard lessons learned during this process will hopefully help him in the future. Finally, a local minority community has had the opportunity to plan and help conduct a relevant environmental education program. This program can help them learn about environmental issues of importance to them and identify resources to help them deal more effectively with environmental problems.

At the present time, it looks like Maryville's future will include two City-Green projects. As a planner, I will try to keep the two planning committees talking to each other, exchanging dialogue, and planning complementary programs. My strategy will be to work with McKee and Wilson, to keep them communicating. I will likely strengthen my relationship with Wilson, in the hope that I can influence him to take a more active role in the development of the Maynard-sponsored CityGreen project. I will encourage the dean to work through Wilson. At the same time, I am continuing to promote the involvement of a variety of city and state leaders in Maynard's planning effort. I feel convinced that a statewide version of the CityGreen project will not address the fundamental issues of environmental justice, environmental education, and environmental literacy. It will become just another mainstream environmental education program. In spite of this, I will work to bring a diversity of viewpoints and voices to the project and to do the best I can under the circumstances.

Learning from Practice

Planning is a political process. To be successful as a planner, risks must always be assumed. Since one can never know in advance the outcome of an action, success is not always predictable. In the Maryville case, my goal was to give community activists a voice in the planning process; I had hoped that their voices would be sufficiently strong to persuade or force traditional power bases to relinquish control or compromise. My intention was not to facilitate the creation of two planning efforts, but that was the practical result. I do not, however, consider this planning effort a failure. It has, like most activities, provided a mixture of advantages and disadvantages to the participants.

One of the primary lessons embedded in this case study is that traditionally silenced voices, in the face of power, must have support to find their voice and their courage. Whether through strength in numbers or through the support of more privileged advocates, low-income and minority residents need a means of challenging entrenched authority figures. This is true even if those figures are also minorities. Government planners often have to provide such support through indirect action. One strategy planners can use to equalize power relationships and encourage a more democratic planning process is to nurture other significant players to act in their place in highly political contexts, as McKee did for me. In nurturing such surrogates, planners may appear to be networking, but in reality they are counteracting.

This clandestine strategy may be the best option for planners whose real interests include promoting a democratic planning process but whose political reality prohibits them from acting directly against those in positions of power. When planners attempt to replace a nondemocratic process with a democratic one, conflict should be anticipated. People in positions of power never give up easily, and in fact they may become more hardened and resolute when challenged. Planners must do everything possible to ensure that challenges to power are backed by sufficient resources. Cervero and Wilson (1994) define power as the capacity to act. Planners can help less powerful players locate whatever resources are available to develop their capacity to act. In the Maryville case, when power successfully turned democracy away, the community group found it had a capacity to act by refusing to participate in the process. This was an act of power. The dean's angry reaction is a testament to the magnitude of that power.

If planners are to act responsibly, they need an ethical vision to guide their judgments in practice. This case study, for example, highlights how planning and education were integral to achieving my vision of environmental justice. Low-income and minority communities are often omitted from the decision-making process. In Maryville, professional politics seemed destined to override the needs and interests of a community that had an obvious need but little political clout. Low-income and minority communities, which bear a disproportionate share of the nation's environmental degradation, are often those with the least knowledge about pollution and what can be done about it. In order to ensure justice in environmental education and environmental literacy, planners must anticipate unequal power relations. Denying powerless communities access to relevant and community-driven environmental education ensures the continued ability of powerful interests to pollute and degrade with impunity. Thus there has often been capitalist opposition to providing environmental education to low-income and minority communities. But environmental justice is not necessarily racially bounded; it may be economically and educationally bounded as well. In the Maryville case, the dean turned racism

on its head, using it as a reason to exclude low-income, minority, and less educated communities from the decision-making process. Future environmental
justice studies should examine the relationship of environmental literacy to
power and influence. Such information would highlight the role of environmental education as a strategy for addressing issues related to environmental
justice and to empower low-income and minority communities to find their
voice in regard to local environmental issues.

Finally, this case study illustrates how planning is itself a learning process.
Through the planning activities for the Maryville CityGreen project, both formal and informal, the participants learned about themselves and about one
another. McKee, for example, was supported in her personal and professional
development as she struggled to find ways to negotiate with the dean. The
dean learned he could be successfully challenged. The community activists
learned they could find their voice. I learned that outcomes can never be
known in advance. Planning, by definition, changes the situation. Planners
should be aware that their actions will have real and lasting consequences, for
those involved in the planning process and for those affected by it. Some of
these changes will be seen as desirable, and others, for the short term at least,
will be seen as deleterious.

Community-based environmental education planning is a complex
process. If planners are to work toward a more substantively democratic planning process, challenges to power are inevitable. In environmental education
and environmental literacy, the stakes are considerable. And so are the rewards.

References

Bullard, R. D. "Overcoming Racism in Environmental Decisionmaking." *Environment*, 1994,
    36 (4), 10–44.
Cervero, R. M., and Wilson, A. L. *Planning Responsibly for Adult Education: A Guide to Nego-
    tiating Power and Interests.* San Francisco: Jossey-Bass, 1994.
Larsen, G., and others. *Synthesis of the Critique of Land Management Planning.* Report no. FS-
    452. Washington, D.C.: USDA Forest Service, 1990.
McArthur, A. A. "Community Partnership—A Formula for Neighborhood Regeneration in
    the 1990s?" *Community Development Journal*, 1993, *28* (4), 305–315.
Sexton, K., Olden, K., and Johnson, B. "Environmental Justice: The Community Role of
    Research in Establishing a Credible Scientific Foundation for Informed Decision Mak-
    ing." *Toxicology and Industrial Health*, 1993, *9* (5), 685–727.
Wals, A.E.J. *Pollution Stinks! Young Adolescents' Perceptions of Nature and Environmental Issues
    with Implications for Education in Urban Settings.* De Lier, The Netherlands: Academic Book
    Center, 1994.

*BARBARA MCDONALD is a social scientist with a federal agency and a doctoral student
in the Department of Adult Education, University of Georgia.*

Empowerment planning is usually depicted as a very organized, placid set of activities. In practice, however, stakeholders with different interests and worldviews employ various strategies to influence planning decisions and outcomes.

How People's Interests Affect Empowerment Planning in a Health Promotion Coalition

Teresa M. Carter

Several theorists in the health promotion field advocate community empowerment as a means of achieving improved quality of life and health. These theorists tend to propose similar techniques for promoting empowerment planning at the community level: (1) enable people in the community to increase their control over important health resources such as knowledge, skills, authority, and money (Green and Raeburn, 1990; Bracht and Kingsbury, 1990); (2) create practical mechanisms for collective decision making so that effective community health education can be targeted to address local health priorities (Braddy, Orenstein, Brownstein, and Cook, 1992; Kreuter, 1992); and (3) enable communities at risk to identify their own prevention and intervention programs, make policy decisions, and identify resources for program implementation (Braithwaite and Lythcott, 1989). The theorists also contend that a successful empowerment planning process is driven by principles of community organization, action, and participation. According to Bracht and Kingsbury (1990), these principles are the "glue" that maintains citizen interest, nourishes participation in programs, and encourages support for long-term maintenance of successful intervention programs.

Empowerment models are based upon a linear set of activities. Bracht and Kingsbury's Community Organization Development (COD) stage model (1990), Kreuter's Planned Approach to Community Health (PATCH) model (1992), and Braithwaite's Coalition Partnership model (1992) all include the following steps: mobilizing or organizing the community; identifying stakeholders; collecting and analyzing data; assessing health issues in the community; and collaborating with stakeholders in the design, planning, implementation, and maintenance of programs. For the most part the models are prescriptive and tend not to portray planning-table dynamics in any detail. Nor do they describe the behaviors of stakeholders, except for the mention of collaborative stakeholder actions. While recognizing that the empowerment planning process seeks to stimulate and coalesce community energies, interests, and resources in a collective response (Bracht and Kingsbury, 1990), the literature does not describe well what health promotion planners really do to achieve empowerment planning. Missing in this discussion is what the stakeholders bring to the table, such as expressed and implied interests, varying and unequal amounts of power, different skill levels and access to resources, and various social and professional relationships and roles. It does not take a leap in logic to see how a consideration of these factors offers immense potential for constructing a more dynamic understanding of the empowerment planning process.

In his discussion of the challenges that face coalitions, Braithwaite (1992, p. 331) accounted for the impact or interplay of such variables in the coalition environment:

> Most potential coalition members convene for different reasons. Some have hidden agendas, while others are fully committed to collaboration for achievement of a common goal. Coalitions should be aware of members who involuntarily "come to the table" because their boss sent them to the organizational meeting. . . . A related concern involves the observation that coalition members may all have one vote but may also face political inequalities based on the influence that a particular member brings to the table. For example, the CEO of the local health department is likely to carry more weight and influence than a low-income, less articulate consumer group member. . . . Under circumstances when the coalition is funded at the beginning of its formation, ulterior motives rooted in financial gain have a way of becoming manifest.

Bogan and his colleagues (1992) provide a critical analysis of an urban PATCH health promotion experience. They posit that implementation of a health promotion program should not be undertaken without paying attention to "a community's sociopolitical dynamics and structure, including key political and community leaders, political ties and positions, agency territorialism, and an existing power structure and prescribed ways of working with the target population" (p. 158). They advise that PATCH partners be knowledgeable about the sociocultural, political, economic, and environmental issues that influence health promotion activities and outcomes in low-income minority communities.

The issues these authors raise suggest that although empowerment planning is depicted as a very organized process, it actually takes place within an environment in which individuals and organizations have intensely differing interests, skills, networks, and power. Recent research by Cervero and Wilson (1994) indicates that planning environments are characterized by interpersonal and interorganizational power relationships marked by differing purposes and interests. The question I pose is, "How do the interests of the planners affect the activities and outcomes of the empowerment planning process?" This chapter uses a case-study analysis of a planning process conducted by an actual coalition of health promotion professionals to establish a minigrant program for health education. I conducted an eleven-month ethnographic study of this particular coalition and its planning process (Carter, 1995), interviewing coalition partners and observing and participating in their planning sessions. In the final stages of this project, I provided technical planning assistance to the coalition.

The Coalition and Major Players

The coalition is located in a large southern city. Formed in 1993 as a six-year collaborative partnership between the Centers for Disease Control (CDC), a local nonprofit social action initiative, and a county health department, the coalition seeks to reduce the county's mortality rate from AIDS and substance abuse. The state commissioner of health spearheaded this coalition in response to a critical need to stem the growing number of such deaths. He created an initiative that would involve the community in the design and implementation of educational programs on HIV, AIDS, and substance abuse. Hence, the coalition was based on the PATCH model, a community participation framework developed by the CDC. Briefly, PATCH is a planning process, adaptable to a variety of situations, that can be used when a community wants to identify and address priority health problems or when a health priority or special population to be addressed has already been selected. The PATCH process helps a community establish a health promotion team, collect and use local data, set health priorities, design interventions, and evaluate their effect (Kreuter, 1992).

I examined the coalition's planning process for the minigrant program to discover the strategies employed by the partners to achieve the coalition's aim of empowerment planning. I selected this process because it provided an excellent opportunity to observe the diversity and interplay of interests and power that the stakeholders brought to the planning table. The conversations, actions, and proposed actions connected with this process provide rich descriptive detail for understanding what happens in the empowerment planning process. A health care agency provided the coalition with funds to make grants to community-based organizations for educational programs on HIV, AIDS, and substance abuse. The coalition had to devise an application procedure; determine criteria for grantees; design the format and content of the application; and determine and arrange the announcement of the minigrants, the call for proposals, the distribution of applications, and the selection and orientation of grantees. The grant amounts ranged from $2,500 to $5,000 and covered a six-month period.

Various political and ethical issues provided a continual backdrop to the planning of the grant-review process; in fact, they often surfaced as centerpieces on the planning table. These issues included the identification of potential grant recipients; the language and content of the grant application; whether grantees should be small, grassroots organizations or established, tax-exempt organizations; and the degree to which proposed programs would be required to reflect the broader aims and goals of the coalition. This chapter examines the positions the coalition partners took on these issues, as well as the strategies they used to influence the planning process.

The following people played integral planning roles. The coalition coordinator, an African-American registered nurse with extensive experience in community organization, has a vast web of grassroots and professional contacts in the local community as well as in the government power structure. She expressed an interest in inviting a "balanced, diverse group of stakeholders" to the planning table, and she used her advocacy and networking skills to invite grassroots organizations and to "ensure that their issues stayed on the table." The public health planner, a European-American public health educator, viewed his role as one of facilitating the PATCH planning process. He has expertise in coalition building and an interest in increasing data-based research on successful models for HIV and substance abuse prevention programs. The physician, an African-American family practitioner and division director within a large county hospital, has worked in several community health agencies and coalitions across the country and has contacts in the medical and academic community. The physician is interested in disease prevention at the community level, because he perceives that treating chronic diseases on an individual basis has negligible results. He agreed with the coordinator that the community's participation and ownership was essential to achieving an improved quality of life. He performed various leadership roles within the coalition (stating that he wanted an opportunity to "run my mouth and hone my group facilitator skills"). The agency director, a European American, heads a large substance abuse education and prevention agency with ties to the public school system and other institutions. His organization conducts research, develops databases on prevention models, and does strategic planning on substance abuse prevention issues. The funding manager, an African American, administers the resources of a state-funded multicounty agency with a focus on funding grassroots organizations to implement primary health care strategies for indigent populations. In March 1994 the funding manager announced to the coalition that she had over $100,000 in minigrant funds for allocation to community-based organizations and that the funds had to be dispersed within four months. She wanted to gain access to organizations "burrowed in local communities" in the county. Her views and interests concerning the inclusion of grassroots organizations in program development merged with the coordinator's perspective.

Political and Ethical Issues

One issue that surfaced repeatedly was the kind of organizations that would be grant recipients. The coalition partners had varying levels of experience with and advocacy for grassroots or community-based organizations. For example, a significant part of the coordinator's background was her extensive experience working with community health partnerships and alliances. She considered the development of relationships with grassroots organizations to be important to the empowerment process. She stated that such relationships were critical to the coalition's efforts because she and her peers really did not understand the worldview of the people directly affected by the health issues the coalition wanted to address. She believed it was important for the coalition to have the input of smaller, neighborhood organizations because "they have the grassroots perspective; they almost always know the real, critical issues, because they are struggling with them themselves."

The funding manager shared the coordinator's views on grassroots participation. Announcing the six-month grants to various community groups attending a coalition meeting at a local church, she said, "People may be sitting around the kitchen table or in the basement of a church with some good ideas and say, 'If we had a thousand dollars we could do this.' These are the kinds of programs, grassroots organizations, we are looking to fund. We encourage innovative ideas and approaches, because this is where the answers, and the best hope for answers, are. It's been proven that we don't have the answers." The coordinator backed up the funding manager by saying, "Please take this information back to your community. We want to fund block groups, grassroots church groups, and so forth."

Thus, informal, grassroots organizations became the targeted grant recipients. The next issue was to ensure that the targeted groups, those that were "burrowed in the community," actually participated in the program. Developing provisions to allow these groups the opportunity to participate involved yet another set of planning decisions. One pivotal decision during the application planning session was to encourage partnerships between nonprofit, 501(c)(3) agencies (a nonprofit, tax-exempt status) and smaller groups that lacked this state certification. Collaboration with 501(c)(3) agencies was discussed with potential grantees that asked whether they had to be 501(c)(3) to qualify for a grant: The physician exclaimed, "That is not fair. Maybe for the integrity of the grant, do it. . . . But it's not fair for smaller organizations." The funding manager replied, "501(c)(3) is not important unless [it is a legal] funding issue. A group could team up with a 501(c)(3) organization. I encourage 'teaming'; it provides a resource exchange."

The decision to encourage collaboration between more established, 501(c)(3) community agencies and smaller, noncharted grassroots organizations was announced at subsequent meetings. A list of 501(c)(3) organizations that were amenable to forming partnerships with grassroots organizations was distributed at the call for proposals meeting. This outcome reflected the fact that the physician and the funding manager were influential in bringing about a key decision that reduced barriers for participation in the program and encouraged inclusion of small, informal grassroots organization. More important, though, were the strategies and sources of power the physician and the funding manager used to influence the resulting decisions.

The coalition partners assumed salient social, professional, and organizational roles that affected the way the affairs of the coalition were conducted. In particular, the physician played very impressive roles both within and apart from the coalition. His physician status and his professional relationships with the coordinator and other major public health players enabled him to play a very significant role within the coalition. He served as a member of the steering committee and as cochair of the goals and objectives committee, and he conducted several planning sessions, including the one on the grant application process. He used his role not only to direct attention to the fairness of including less-formal groups but also to prompt discussions of alternatives such as the 501(c)(3) partnerships. These partnerships had the desired impact of permitting the inclusion of organizations "burrowed into the community," which was his expressed interest.

For her part, the funding manager used her economic power to develop collaborative relationships and to satisfy her interests in the planning process. The 501(c)(3) partnerships were her idea, and they eventually became an integral part of the planning strategy. Also, the relationship the funding manager forged with the coordinator more than likely "greased the planning wheels." The basis of their relationship converged on a set of needs or expectations. The funding manager was seeking grassroots organizations with innovative strategies to whom she could award minigrants, and the coordinator was looking for a "carrot" to get community groups to buy into the coalition. Needless to say, their relationship enabled both of these women to achieve their professional aims and interests. The funding manager secured her relationship with the coordinator and the coalition through economic power, and the coordinator used the power of her position to bring the funding manager to the planning table and thus give her access to potential grantees.

Another very pivotal issue was revealed in the stakeholders' discussions about the content and format of the grant application. Some members, particularly the public health planner, wanted to ensure that the PATCH model would be used in establishing criteria, but the funding manager cautioned that the language must be user-friendly to grassroots organizations. Parenthetically, the stakeholders all agreed that grantees should be required to incorporate the coalition's goals and objectives into their programs. What was at issue was whether the application's comprehensiveness would be compromised by its research orientation. As the funding manager asked in a planning meeting, "Are we scaring away people who can really do these programs? We want the process to be inclusive."

It was clear that the agency director and the public health planner were "on the same page" regarding this issue. For example, the agency director's suggestions for application procedures and for the wording and construction of the application were favorably received by the public health planner. They had similar ideas about the application's content as well. The case study data suggested certain parallels and interconnections in their respective attempts to influence planning decisions. For example, the agency director shared research on the benefits of considering risk factors for various diseases in planning a community health education program; this information influenced many planning decisions concerning program development criteria. Risk-factor information was valued by the public health planner as well, because it is central to the PATCH process. Thus, the agency director's ability to influence the process was derived from his knowledge and expertise, and these attributes formed the basis of his partnership with the public health planner and other coalition members. In fact, the agency director's knowledge heavily influenced the focus of the planning group as well as the application package it produced. It is arguable whether or not the agency director's and the public health planner's common interests, expertise, vision for the application, and professional goals (to develop long-range solutions to substance abuse problems) formed the basis of their collaborative relationship. But it is clear that their relationship and expertise influenced the development of the minigrant application procedures.

To reiterate, the discussions about the construction of the application showed that some coalition partners primarily wanted to keep the application simple, while others were more concerned with ensuring that it buttressed the funding criteria. Their exchanges also revealed the ethical issues at the center of the planning effort. Clearly, interests were negotiated, because the resulting grant application and other decisions indicate that the different stakeholders were able to achieve their desired outcomes. The eventual application was user-friendly, limited to ten pages and asking questions that did not require lengthy answers. It was oriented toward encouraging programs that would reduce various risk factors for disease, and it stipulated that the coalition's goals and objectives were to be followed in developing program designs. The final application reflected negotiated decisions, evidencing that the stakeholders' exercise of power had an impact on the planning process. The emergence of issues seemed to serve as catalysts for the employment of various tactics and strategies by the stakeholders to influence decisions, cement relationships, and advance interests. In sum, the partners' exercise of power to advance their interests drove this empowerment planning scenario.

Learning from Practice

Given what has been discovered in this case study, there is arguably significantly more tension and noise in the coalition planning environment than previously accounted for by Bracht and Kingsbury (1990) and Braithwaite (1992). We can now return to the question posed initially: "How do the interests of the planners affect the activities and outcomes of the empowerment planning process?" I can argue that empowerment planning did take place in that a core of interested persons came together; collected, reviewed, and analyzed data; identified AIDS and substance abuse as critical causes of premature death among the community's residents; and explored alternative strategies for prevention. When the minigrant funds became available, the coalition partners, through a series of planning activities, constructed a minigrant application process that led to the funding of community-based organizations for the implementation of HIV and substance abuse prevention and intervention programs. The empowerment planning process steps were followed, but a lot of other stuff happened too.

What I learned is that during this collaborative decision-making process, certain political and ethical issues became central. The partners had differing views on how the community and other interests should be represented or served. For example, the public health planner's interest in fulfilling the PATCH formula was represented by his proposing a research-focused grant application. Also, the grassroots organizations' interests were represented in their inclusion as the preferred targets for the grants. Thus, the planners took positions on issues, proposed options, wielded whatever power they had, and negotiated among various interests to bring about their desired outcomes. I observed that people did not necessarily negotiate around or collaborate on specific educational programs per se; rather, they negotiated around the issues that came up as they conceptualized and constructed the program. People tend to respond to and interact with issues and to take appropriate action according to their positions on these issues. I think that the eventual result of this planning process illustrates how planners work through the various political and ethical issues on the planning table. Out of the resolution of these issues comes the concrete program design, which determines what or who will participate in or be affected by the program, and when.

This research may serve to alert health promotion or education program planners that when people come together to plan programs, they first of all plan around issues. Through this process they influence the planning decisions and they influence each other; likewise, they are influenced or empowered by their actions, interactions, and interrelationships. Although these behaviors are consistently demonstrated by people in planning contexts, they can present daunting challenges to planning practitioners. As planning practitioners we must be prepared to pay attention to these dynamic factors in the coalition environment as well as to the elements of traditional empowerment planning models. We should be aware of those situations in which interests and issues, as well as the ability to influence, may not always facilitate the empowerment objectives of the planning process. In fact, it is very likely that planning, in particular empowerment planning, will get lost or subverted in the complex interplay of power relationships, interests, and sociostructural and economic factors present in such environments. Thus, educators bent on empowering communities must work with the participants and direct their attention toward strategies that will ensure that community interests are adequately represented at the planning table. This must occur for the resultant programs to offer tangible benefits to community life.

References

Bogan, G., and others. "Organizing an Urban African-American Community for Health Promotion: Lessons from Chicago." *Journal of Health Education,* 1992, *23* (3), 157–159.

Bracht, N., and Kingsbury, L. "Community Organization Principles in Health Promotion." In N. Bracht (ed.), *Health Promotion at the Community Level.* Thousand Oaks, Calif.: Sage, 1990.

Braddy, B., Orenstein, D., Brownstein, J. N., and Cook, T. "PATCH: An Example of Community Empowerment for Health." *Journal of Health Education,* 1992, *23* (3), 179–182.

Braithwaite, R. "Coalition Partnerships for Health Promotion." In R. Braithwaite and S. Taylor (eds.), *Health Issues in the Black Community.* San Francisco: Jossey-Bass, 1992.

Braithwaite, R., and Lythcott, N. "Community Empowerment as a Strategy for Health Promotion for Black and Other Minority Populations." *Journal of the American Medical Association,* 1989, *261* (2), 282–283.

Carter, T. M. "Factors in a Health Promotion Coalition That Impact Program Planning for Empowerment." Unpublished doctoral dissertation, Department of Adult Education, University of Georgia, 1995.

Cervero, R. M., and Wilson, A. L. *Planning Responsibly for Adult Education: A Guide to Negotiating Power and Interests.* San Francisco: Jossey-Bass, 1994.

Green, L., and Raeburn, J. "Contemporary Developments in Health Promotion." In N. Bracht (ed.), *Health Promotion at the Community Level.* Thousand Oaks, Calif.: Sage, 1990.

Kreuter, M. "PATCH: Its Origin, Basic Concepts, and Links to Contemporary Public Health Policy." *Journal of Health Education,* 1992, *23* (3), 135–139.

TERESA M. CARTER is cofounder of Carter & Elbert Consultants. She conducts research and provides training and technical assistance in community health assessment and health promotion planning in Georgia.

Perceiving the power and interests inherent in an apparently
everyday setting—a nursing education program—is critical
in order to effect meaningful and desired change.

Renegotiating Institutional Power Relationships to Better Serve Nursing Students

Susan M. Hendricks

Early one evening, while looking out from a dock on Big Mantrap Lake, it occurred to me that describing program planning in nursing education was quite a bit like looking at the lake. What I saw that evening, miles away from the nursing school, was the calm surface of the water and the glint of the late-day sun reflected on it. There were only a few ripples disturbing the surface, and to my right some lily pads were floating quietly. But underneath this apparently serene surface, a dynamic ecosystem of negotiated power and interests created a constantly changing environment. When considering program planning for nursing students, I realized that those things on the surface—educational topics and objectives, timing and details of programs, and even teaching strategies—are less important than the interplay of structural and personal interests and power relationships underneath. Beneath the surface of the lake there is earth: rocky, muddy, sandy; always present and always influencing life in the lake. There are plants and fish. Power relationships permeate life under the surface. Minnows, crappies, and northern pike: each holds a distinct position of power in relation to the other. Describing the structural and interpersonal interests and power relationships in a nursing education program, which is like describing the life under the surface of a lake, offers an opportunity to define and clarify what matters in planning programs for nurses.

Educational Program Planning in Nursing

Program planners in nursing education often approach their practice from a position up on the dock, focusing almost entirely on educational goals, objectives, and teaching strategies. Rarely do they recognize or articulate the dynamic interactions that occur under the surface. Yet it is the dynamics of power and interests that really determine the educational plans created by nursing educators. The field of nursing has been heavily influenced by the wave of logical positivism that engulfed most of the social sciences during the twentieth century. This influence permeates every aspect of nursing, from bedside care to nursing research (Wilson-Thomas, 1995). In fact, nursing practice is defined by the "nursing process," taught nearly universally as the method for practicing as a registered nurse. The nursing process consists of a series of steps paralleling the steps of the scientific method.

Therefore, not surprisingly, within nursing education, most authors describe program planning as a series of steps (Wassel, 1994). Perhaps the most influential group in defining nursing education is the National League for Nursing (NLN), which accredits schools of nursing nationwide. In a major attempt to develop and define the field, the NLN has set forth specific measurable objectives for use in accrediting schools. These criteria tie nursing education to a Tylerian frame of reference (National League for Nursing, 1990; Tyler, 1949). For many years, experts in the field of nursing curriculum development, such as Bevis (1982) and Scales (1985), expertly argued for an objectives-driven approach. In recent years, Bevis and Watson (1989) and the National League for Nursing (1993) have concluded that in order to move forward, nursing education must move beyond this behaviorist paradigm in favor of a more humanistic position. However, with the NLN criteria currently in place, such a significant paradigm shift has not materialized. Furthermore, even though the promoters of this new humanistic perspective discuss what the curriculum plans for the future of nursing education should look like, there is little emphasis placed on the interpersonal process of planning for nursing education.

There has been a steady, small movement within nursing to question the perspective of logical positivism as a basis for practice and to address the interpersonal power dynamics involved. This movement originated with nurses using qualitative and feminist research approaches (Henderson, 1995). For example, Hewison (1995) studied nurses' power in interactions with patients, using a participant-observation approach that focused heavily on how language and power relationships are connected. Strategies for negotiating power and interests have been addressed by a few nursing authors. The need for collaborative relationships within nursing has been described by Henneman, Lee, and Cohen (1995). These authors posited that through collaborative efforts, patient outcomes improve. In nursing education, Congdon and French (1995) described the development of collegial relationships among nursing faculty in the United Kingdom. Further thoughtful inquiry is needed to articulate the negotiation of power and interests in the context of nursing curriculum planning.

Cervero and Wilson (1994) have described a theory of program planning practice intended to assist planners to "responsibly negotiate interests in organizational relationships of power" (p. 115). The thrust of the theory is that "pragmatic planners must be able to read organizational power relationships in order to anticipate conflict and provide support in carrying out a vision of planning that is substantively democratic" (p. 115). Four main ideas are clearly identified: power, interests, negotiation, and responsibility. Cervero and Wilson's theory provides a much needed link between the NLN's vision of a reformed nursing educational system and the NLN's actual practice. The purpose of this chapter, then, is to describe the politics of planning practice in nursing education, such as within the Nursing Achievement Program.

The Nursing Achievement Program

Reflecting on the glassy surface of Big Mantrap Lake, it is easy to be lulled into thinking that the lake is simple and quiescent. Similarly, the small, nondescript Nursing Achievement Program (NAP), part of a University-based nursing school in a small midwestern city, seems almost too quiet a context for addressing concepts such as the negotiation of power and interests. However, such a seemingly quiet program, when examined carefully, offers a rich opportunity for the examination and appreciation of Cervero and Wilson's theoretical perspectives. Negotiation of power and interests occurs at all levels: not only in the grand aspects of program planning, but also among the everyday communications of educational planners.

NAP, which is supported by a Perkins grant, has the goal of promoting academic success for students pursuing an associate of science degree in Nursing. Many of our students have little experience in higher education. Many are women with limited economic resources and multiple responsibilities. NAP seeks to help students become registered nurses. The program director reports directly to the nursing school dean. The program is categorized as a support service. The faculty and administration at the university assume that NAP serves the needs of associate degree students and thereby promotes their academic success. Since our activities fit easily within this realm, we are supported by these groups. Faculty frequently make referrals to the program and are supportive of our programming for students. Although consensus regarding our purpose is high, NAP does not have much power within the nursing school or the university at large. For example, the program is rarely represented in groups with decision-making authority. Our lack of authority serves to bring us closer to students, since we are not seen as holding any influence over them. Furthermore, we offer little threat to the established power bases within the nursing school, so we have been accepted easily. The disadvantage to this position lies in our reliance on persuasion and networking, both with students and faculty, to accomplish our goals. This seems to be a common phenomenon among programs supported by grant monies. Being funded by a grant, NAP has questionable longevity and authority.

There are four part-time positions in the program. The coordinator position is a part-time responsibility for the director of nursing continuing education. Our coordinator is a helpful, quiet individual who mainly functions as an administrative liaison. Though she holds some formal positional power, the coordinator manages the program by assuming that each member of the staff can and will manage his or her own responsibilities within the program. The coordinator's interests are for NAP to function well. Her philosophy of management is also an interest of hers, being decidedly nondirective. She has worked for the university for many years and has a working awareness of how to approach and deal with most interactions with others in the university.

The academic counselor is a half-time position, held by a counselor with a master's degree. The academic counselor aligns herself heavily with the nursing administration office and seems to have some difficulty focusing her time on NAP's mission. This may have to do with the fact that when she began as a fledgling professional in this position several years ago, the dean at the time had limited the scope of her counseling activities significantly. With the arrival of a new dean, this restrictive atmosphere has dissipated. However, the academic counselor has not developed into an active performer in her role. It seems as if her main interests involve protecting the power she has acquired through her association with the administrative department of the nursing school. She has remained distant from the program and the students.

The science tutor is a half-time position held by a former premed student who decided to teach literature after she completed a degree in zoology. The science tutor is well regarded by students and has been productive in the program. She is approachable and understanding. This was the science tutor's first professional position. Initially she was fairly passive and unassuming. Gradually, she has grown to be an assertive student advocate. The science tutor's interest in student advocacy stems from her own experience with oppression and her transformation from an attitude of passivity.

I am the nursing tutor, a position that represents 40 percent of my responsibilities at the university. My perspective on helping nursing students is grounded in my experience as a nursing program planner and faculty member. I am an assertive member of NAP and am reasonably productive at meeting student's needs. My primary interest was to develop NAP into a program that operates effectively to meet students' educational needs. From past experience in program planning, I was acutely aware that every aspect of how the program operates would influence our effectiveness with students. I saw that our location, our legitimacy, and our collegiality would all affect how helpful we would be to students. My efforts "under the surface" kept these aims in mind.

Networking: Establishing Symmetrical Power Relationships

Because NAP lacked a central location and its staff members were dispersed, the program was not serving the students' needs as well as it should. To improve the service, several specific strategies were employed in an effort to establish symmetrical power relationships within the program: renegotiating physical space arrangements, creating a team-oriented milieu, and developing a mutual planning project to facilitate maximum efficacy of all program members.

Acquiring a Space. NAP's history played a role in how its power relationships developed. When I began as the nursing tutor in the summer of 1994, the NAP "program" was composed of four individuals with little in common. The previous nursing tutor had operated out of a classroom and a file cabinet. The science tutor worked from a desk and file cabinet in an alcove. The academic counselor's office was in the nursing administration area in the school of nursing. Within this office was the program's single telephone. The coordinator's office was on another floor in the same building. Thus, all program members were physically isolated from one another.

This physical arrangement was problematic for several reasons: first, students needed a place to identify with as the program's home. "Having a place" was crucial to establishing the program's legitimacy and to making it available to the nursing school and university communities. Second, the dispersed arrangement offered no opportunity for collaboration among program members. Third, the placement of the phone effectively limited its usefulness to the academic counselor. This reinforced an inappropriate distribution of power within the program, giving excess power and increased accessibility to the academic counselor. These physical arrangements had far-reaching effects, keeping us from networking effectively with students, faculty, and one another.

Recognizing this as a primary problem, I first discussed the situation with the science tutor. I was aware that she held some of the same concerns that I did. Because we were in agreement that NAP needed a more permanent location, we formed an alliance. The academic counselor had no interest in joining us—she had an office right next to the dean. When the science tutor and I brought our request to the attention of the coordinator, she was agreeable and began to make initial inquiries regarding space. Initially we were put off by the university administration because of a limitation in available office space.

The science tutor and I began to forage around the university and located several areas that were not being used—a few small office areas and a large computer lab that had recently been vacated. At this point we repeated our request, with these specific locations noted on our request. We began to articulate more clearly the reasons for our persistence. This "cause" forged a solid working relationship between us. Finally, we were granted the use of the vacant computer room for one academic year. Realizing that once we had a place we were likely to become a more visible entity, we felt sure that we were off to a productive start. Once we had settled into our new space, the benefits became evident. Students dropped by more often, appointments increased, and the science tutor and I began to share ideas about our practice in a collegial manner. We began to develop a legitimate power base within the university. As the year progressed, our room became the location for multiple workshops, study groups, and individual appointments. Still, the academic counselor remained removed from the thrust of the program, partially due to her physical location.

Creating a Team-Oriented Milieu. While this change in physical location served to bring the science tutor and myself into a working alliance, we remained isolated from the academic counselor. Several factors seemed to play a part. When the program began, several years before, the science tutor was new to holding a professional position and was thus very passive. The dean at the time encouraged this behavior. The academic counselor survived this oppressive atmosphere by aligning herself with other persons on the nursing administration staff. Unfortunately, a rift developed between the science tutor and the academic counselor. The science tutor described feeling belittled by the academic counselor and grew resentful. The academic counselor remained aloof from NAP's emerging role in our new location. There was an unspoken tension present that was almost palpable.

As NAP solidified into a more team-oriented effort, the academic counselor's lack of focus on the program's mission became more evident. In an effort to draw the four of us together, we began to meet weekly. During our weekly meetings we shared our activities and began to plan some joint efforts. Perhaps the idea of holding regular meetings is obvious, but prior to this point, meetings with all of the program staff were very rare. In a program that is tightly budgeted, time spent collaborating is often the first to be eliminated. Through our regular meetings, however, we were able to begin to address some of the interpersonal issues that seemed to be getting in the way of providing services to students.

Though our weekly meetings were productive, the academic counselor continued to provide few direct student services. The tension between the science tutor and the academic counselor seemed quite insurmountable. It became apparent to me that the academic counselor needed to become a team member, more dedicated to student success, and networking alone would not accomplish this goal. Since my position was in a peer relationship with the academic counselor, it was not my place to dictate where she located her office. Instead, I began to voice the fact that there was ample room in our vacated computer lab for the academic counselor to have an office. Fortunately, both the coordinator for NAP and the new dean seemed to be aware of some of these issues. The academic counselor was asked to plan to move into the NAP office space during the next summer break. This move would enhance accessibility to students, I reasoned. Realizing that I was not likely to be successful in directly tackling the tense relationship between the science tutor and the academic counselor, I began to think in terms of drawing the academic counselor into a productive, student-centered relationship with me. In effect, I attempted to draw the academic counselor into a collaborative relationship directly with me, circumventing the conflict between the academic counselor and the science tutor altogether.

Altering Power Relationships. Recognizing that working with others successfully on a collaborative project can draw individuals together as a team, I began to think about initiating a project that might serve this purpose as well as address students' needs. At a staff meeting in February 1995, we began to discuss a workshop for incoming nursing students that would provide preliminary guidance regarding the unique challenges and stresses involved in the program. We had done a workshop for new students before, and it had met with great success. The academic counselor had recently received positive feedback regarding her performance in meeting her responsibilities within the grant's focus, and she seemed eager to engage in a student-centered project. The timing was good; all it took was a small suggestion that we consider doing a workshop together.

Once we had decided to go ahead with a workshop for incoming nursing students, there were several decisions to be made. This process of negotiation provided an opportunity for us to forge mutual relationships and negotiate differences in a satisfying manner. The first decision we discussed was timing. Since all of the positions within NAP are part-time, we all have other pressing responsibilities. Through a friendly negotiation process, we attempted to consider the needs and wants of the learners as we saw them, and we also worked within our own time constraints. We used feedback from last year's workshop to determine that whole-day sessions were not desirable. Finally, we decided on two consecutive mornings late in May. We altered the time of year for the workshop from late June to late May with no real recognition that this might affect student involvement. Looking back, this decision was a significant enough change that seeking feedback from students about it would have been wise. During this process, we considered the voices of students, teachers, and planners. Less thought was given to the responses of nursing faculty, administration, or the larger public. However, there was a high degree of consensus regarding our mission among the faculty and administration, and it conformed to the intent of the grant as well.

Choosing the topics for the workshops involved a very short discussion, yet there was a clear effort to create some bridges with nursing faculty through our choices. We used the four topics that had been used at last year's workshop: reading and study skills, test taking, memory aids, and stress management. These topics represented needs students had consistently voiced. We asked a faculty member to present on memory aids. By including a representative faculty stakeholder in the program, this action created a bridge between NAP and the nursing faculty. After some discussion, we decided to use a new speaker, also a member of the nursing faculty, for the stress management topic. It was during our discussion about this speaker that the science tutor gave her only opinion about what ought to happen at the workshop: "You know, a lot of the students were put off by the speaker we had last year. She came across so perfect and like she was so far above everyone else that it was a real downer." Beyond this comment, the science tutor remained removed from any involvement in this workshop. It seemed at the time that her withdrawal from program planning was designed to avoid direct conflict. Certainly, asking nursing faculty to join us in presenting this workshop served to strengthen our rapport with the faculty.

One of the more significant decisions we made concerning this workshop was to initiate some small group sessions. The academic counselor had purchased several new videos for use with students, and she wanted a chance to try them out. I wanted to try something new that might be useful to the students, without risking an entire workshop on an unproven approach. We decided to offer small group break-out sessions, offering students the option of viewing the new videos and incorporating a piece on managing time that I had been considering for several weeks. These sessions would also allow students to give us some direct and specific feedback about their wants and needs. The coordinator, the academic counselor, and I agreed to each handle one small group session.

After our initial discussions and decisions, our planning meetings consisted largely of checking in with one another regarding details of planning practice: room arrangements, flyers, and contracts for outside speakers. This moved along quite smoothly and reinforced a team spirit. The workshop was a moderate success, both in the responses of students and in our emerging relationships within NAP. There were less participants than in the previous year, though essentially all of the students who attended spoke positively about the workshop. The academic counselor remains somewhat removed from NAP, though she seems to be congenial and is willing to be involved in future projects.

Learning from Practice

In looking at the planning process for the workshop for incoming students, defining the students' learning needs and developing the workshop's topics and objectives was only the surface of the lake—familiar, but without depth. Underneath the surface of the lake called educational programming there is a dynamic, changing environment composed of power relationships, negotiated interests, and ethical issues. Every communication that occurs among members of NAP and with various stakeholders in the program influences the future power relationships in the program. Being aware of these dynamics is essential to good planning practice. The planner who is aware of the possible effect of these everyday communications has the ability to bring about change and create programs that develop in meaningful, desired directions.

Beneath the process of hammering out the specific details of the workshop, the power relationships among the planners both influenced and were influenced by our communications. A part of the workshop plan related to my goal of bringing the academic counselor to an awareness of the power she has in her position to serve the students. As the members of NAP completed projects together successfully, we became partners, a more symmetrical power relationship. A somewhat similar situation is described by Congdon and French (1995) in their analysis of the development of collaborative collegiality among a changing environment for nursing faculty in the United Kingdom. The students ultimately benefit.

Beneath the surface of a lake, many forms of life interact according to their interests: eating, breathing, reproducing. Within the realm of program planning, Cervero and Wilson (1994) suggest that people seek to serve their interests by responding in certain ways to various situations and by positioning themselves in relationship to others. In this case study, each of the four members of NAP held certain interests relating to this workshop. My actions as a nursing tutor may have appeared to be simple efforts at planning a workshop for new nursing students. While this was a part of my intention, underneath the surface I was attempting to renegotiate the way the members of NAP worked together, to bring about a collaborative, team-oriented program with maximum student benefit.

The creatures living in a lake engage in negotiations: swimming in schools, avoiding predators, confronting rivals. Cervero and Wilson note that "planners work with people to construct programs, and their negotiations take a variety of forms, ranging from informal discussions to well-structured practical strategies and techniques" (p. 156). During the planning of the workshop, negotiation was evident. There was a high degree of consensus regarding some of the decisions, such as the topics for the main presentations. Other decisions required more discussion, such as the issue of dates and times for the workshop. Even the tendency of the planners to stay out of certain aspects of the planning was an act of negotiation. Compared with other planning activities I have been involved with, planning this workshop seemed to be characterized by a high degree of consensus—it was clearly a "win-win" situation for the three of us who were involved.

Within the lake, each change that occurs subtly influences the balance of life. As planners, we are responsible for representing differing interests democratically. Ethics is important, helping the planner answer the question "What for?" rather than simply "How?" (Cervero and Wilson, 1994, p. 137). This value position is what gives direction to the planner's work. Cervero and Wilson argue that the responsible planner should democratize the planning process by including the voices or perspectives of five groups: learners, teachers, planners, institutional leadership, and the public. Because the thoughtful planner has a responsibility to effect meaningful change, defining what is meaningful in planning practice becomes essential. The educational planner, then, has a responsibility to each of the stakeholders in the program. For NAP these stakeholders included nursing and prenursing students, the public, the faculty, the nursing school and university administration, and the NAP program members. With a high degree of consensus among nursing faculty, the current administration, the students, and NAP programmers regarding the purpose and goals of NAP, the most significant issues regarding representation of interests related to enhancing the participation of the academic counselor in addressing student needs.

Out on the dock at Big Mantrap, the evening sun began to sink behind the trees. The absence of the sun's glare made it easier to look beneath the surface.

The closer I looked, the more I saw. Experience and reflection on the nature of program planning under the surface facilitate recognition of the dynamic nature of the negotiation of power and interests in educational program planning, even in the quietest of landscapes.

References

Bevis, E. *Curriculum Building in Nursing: A Process.* (3rd ed.) St. Louis: Mosby, 1982.

Bevis, E., and Watson, J. *Toward a Caring Curriculum: A New Pedagogy in Nursing.* New York: National League for Nursing, 1989.

Cervero, R. M., and Wilson, A. L. *Planning Responsibly for Adult Education: A Guide to Negotiating Power and Interests.* San Francisco: Jossey-Bass, 1994.

Congdon, G., and French, P. "Collegiality, Adaptation, and Nursing Faculty." *Journal of Advanced Nursing,* 1995, *21,* 748–758.

Henderson, D. J. "Consciousness Raising in Participatory Research: Method and Methodology for Emancipatory Nursing Inquiry." *Advances in Nursing Science,* 1995, *17* (3), 58–69.

Henneman, E., Lee, J., and Cohen, J. "Collaboration: A Concept Analysis." *Journal of Advanced Nursing,* 1995, *21,* 103–109.

Hewison, A. "Nurses' Power in Interactions with Patients." *Journal of Advanced Nursing,* 1995, *21,* 75–82.

National League for Nursing. *Policies and Procedures of Accreditation in Nursing Education.* (6th ed.) New York: Division of Education and Accreditation, National League for Nursing, 1990.

National League for Nursing. *A Vision for Nursing Education.* New York: National League for Nursing, 1993.

Scales, F. *Nursing Curriculum: Development, Structure, and Function.* Englewood Cliffs, N.J.: Appleton-Century-Crofts, 1985.

Tyler, R. *Basic Principles of Curriculum and Instruction.* Chicago: University of Chicago Press, 1949.

Wassel, M. "Successful Educational Activities in Nursing." *AAOHN Journal,* 1994, *42* (9), 425–434.

Wilson-Thomas, L. "Applying Critical Social Theory in Nursing Education to Bridge the Gap Between Theory, Research, and Practice." *Journal of Advanced Nursing,* 1995, *21,* 568–575.

SUSAN M. HENDRICKS is visiting lecturer in nursing at Indiana University, Kokomo.

*Program planners need to be aware of the purpose of continuing
professional education in their organization and the organization's
expectations for it. One purpose that continuing medical education
may serve is to expand the clinical practice of an institution
by generating patient referrals from community-based
primary care physicians.*

Negotiating Between Competing Interests in Planning Continuing Medical Education

Roger G. Maclean

The national health care system has gone through major changes in the past several years, particularly with the advent of managed care. These changes have affected the role that continuing medical education (CME) plays in university-based institutions and how the CME program planner meets both the internal and external needs of those institutions. Cervero (1984) identifies referrals as a key strategy for obtaining intangible resources in order to ensure a medical center's long-term survival. Referral relationships are more easily developed from the position of power and prestige provided by a university medical center. They help ensure a continuous flow of participants for a university medical center's programs and hopefully increase the number of patients referred to its clinical practice centers. The majority of CME program planning literature (Brown and Uhl, 1970; Mazmanian, 1980; Moore, 1984; Sork, 1990) does not recognize or address this issue, however. This case study looks at the importance of referrals and how planners must negotiate power relationships to serve both internal and external interests.

Brown and Uhl (1970) developed the "bi-cycle" concept, which relates patient care to learning and education. This model was the first to emphasize the interaction between the patient and the physician-learner and the importance it plays in determining patient needs rather than simply serving the interests of the program planner or instructor. The final evaluation of success is based on whether or not the patient's needs have been met. The purpose of the model was to move CME from a process of information transfer to more of a problem-solving approach; as such, it was quite different from the traditional

NEW DIRECTIONS FOR ADULT AND CONTINUING EDUCATION, no. 69, Spring 1996 © Jossey-Bass Publishers approach to CME program planning. Moore (1984) and Walsh (1984) both emphasize the importance of this model and the fact that the ultimate purpose of these programs is to improve the quality of patient care. Walsh goes on to say that hospital administrators may want confirmation that these programs have an effect on the performance and competence of physicians that results in improved patient care in order to justify their cost. Sork (1990) also notes the "bi-cycle" model and states that planning must begin with an assessment of the quality of patient care and that evaluation should be based on measuring improvement in that quality. He adds that being aware of the political, economic, and social climate of one's institution is important because of the effect it has on the planning process.

Most of the previously cited literature concludes that the primary role of CME programs is to improve patient care and to update the skills of practitioners, with the intent of increasing quality. This certainly meets an internal need of health care institutions and serves the interest of patients. But another, evolving need that these programs serve is to increase referrals from primary care physicians so that the clinical practice increases, specialists are kept working, beds are full, and operating rooms are busy. With the advent of managed care and the increasing popularity of health maintenance organizations (HMOs) and preferred provider organizations (PPOs), the community-based family practice physician has become an important source of business for the specialists practicing at university medical centers. These primary care physicians are the initial point of contact for the patient, and they decide at what point and to whom the patient should be referred when specialized care is required.

Mazmanian (1980) describes what he calls "social structural forces" and the effect they have on the program development process. He further subdivides these forces into internal and external categories. One of the internal forces he notes is the cost of maintaining a CME unit and the fact that these units are considered self-supporting and work on a cost-recovery basis. External forces include cosponsorship of activities with other professional organizations, such as rural community-based hospitals, and requests from informal groups of practicing physicians, such as primary care providers. His approach recognizes the influence that both internal and external groups may have on the program planning process. Cervero (1984) specifically identifies the importance of collaborating with external agencies in order to increase referrals to a medical school's teaching hospitals and clinics. This informal referral relationship also benefits the CME unit by increasing the number of professionals who attend its programs. As a provider of CME, the university-based medical center has a unique position of power and prestige in its relationship with the community hospital. This power allows the medical center to provide programs that not only have the potential to improve the quality of patient care but also can serve as a marketing tool to expand its clinical services. This increase in clinical services may outweigh the need to recover all expenses associated with the CME program and may actually serve to subsidize its costs.

Cervero and Wilson (1994) state that planners work with a variety of interpersonal and institutional interests that affect the final program design. This necessitates that planners be aware of the power relationships and the interests to be served, both internally and externally, and be able to promote their own specific interests as well as negotiate between the interests of the others involved in the planning process. In this case, the planners' expressed interests might be to educate professionals about a new procedure and to improve the quality of care, while their real interest might be to increase patient referrals. Planners need this type of knowledge in order to deliver a program that meets the expectations of all involved.

A Continuing Medical Education Case Study

This case study is based on a total of nine audiotaped interviews completed over a three-month period with the associate dean for continuing medical education and external affairs, the director of continuing education, and three program coordinators at a university-based medical school. The names of the institution and the people have been changed to maintain confidentiality. The purpose of this case study is to describe the administrative structure of the continuing education function at the medical school and the CME program's relationship to the university and its external clients. This will provide a better understanding of the political environment within the institution, the various levels of power present there, and how they are negotiated.

Eastern University is a comprehensive, multicampus research university that serves the needs of its state. Its land-grant mission includes instruction, research, and community service and requires responsiveness to and support from both the public and private sectors. The Department of Continuing Education delivers programs both for internal staff and faculty and for external health care professionals. The department provides CME outreach and programs for thirteen regional hospitals, collaborates in educational development and resource sharing with three affiliated hospitals and one partner hospital, and implements speaker contracts and resource support for an additional eight regional hospitals. Eastern University is accredited by the Accreditation Council for Continuing Medical Education (ACCME) to sponsor continuing medical education for physicians. The College of Medicine is actively negotiating several formal affiliation agreements with community hospitals that will include providing all or a major portion of those hospitals' continuing education needs for all health care professionals. These agreements have the potential to reduce costs for the community hospitals, but they also pose a threat to their existing continuing education staff, who may be eliminated or reduced to part-time status. There are additional potential benefits to the hospitals, including shared services and diagnostic equipment and increased purchasing power for medical supplies. The College of Medicine is located one hundred miles south of Eastern University's main campus, in a small rural community in the center of the state.

The dean of the College of Medicine reports to the president of the university and has minimal involvement in the day-to-day activities of the Department of Continuing Education. He sits on several prominent national professional association boards, however, and therefore has been able to identify some upcoming important national programs in need of a CME sponsor and direct them to Eastern University's College of Medicine. His political clout on the national scene has allowed the university to capitalize on opportunities that otherwise may not have come its way.

Greg is the associate dean for continuing medical education and external affairs, a part-time administrative position within continuing education. In addition, he is a full-time faculty member and a department chair. Department chairs in the College of Medicine hold significant power within the institution and are considered to be at a level even with the associate dean. Without this status, Greg would have limited power and authority in his role as associate dean, particularly with the departments that generate significant revenue for the hospital, such as surgery and cardiology. Additional power comes from the fact that he is a member of the dean's executive council, a small, twelve-member inner circle that advises the dean. His key responsibilities include helping the CME unit maintain academic links with all of the faculty, expanding the presence of the medical center beyond the campus by identifying CME opportunities in the external environment, and negotiating in politically difficult situations that may occur between departments and faculty and the Department of Continuing Education.

Dave is the director of continuing education for the College of Medicine and is administratively, academically, and financially responsible to the dean. He reports directly to Greg, the associate dean. He also has a reporting line to the dean and vice president of continuing education, who is located at the main campus. This reporting line is primarily for administrative support, such as for reporting problems with the university's registration and records system; Dave's position does not directly influence academic matters. Instead, Dave's role within the College of Medicine is purely administrative and involves such things as processing course approvals, maintaining a course record system, and assigning course numbers to those programs offered. In addition, he coordinates the Continuing Education Liaison Committee (CELC), which is the academic review committee for continuing education programs sponsored by the College of Medicine. The CELC has representatives from each of the clinical and basic science departments, hospital administration, and nursing. The committee reviews all program approval requests. Once approved, the Department of Continuing Education conducts the program. Dave also supervises three program coordinators, who have individual responsibility for physician programs, nursing programs, and allied health programs. Greg also sees Dave as being responsible for educating the faculty of the College of Medicine on how to be more successful at CME and for introducing new and creative ideas and technologies that will extend the college's programming to the external professional health care community.

The department is organized into four teams, each with an assigned area of program responsibility. Each team is responsible for mastering the requirements of its area and those of the accreditation process. Currently the four teams are physician CME, nursing, allied health, and outreach. These teams consist of a program coordinator and a staff assistant. Carol is the program coordinator for physician CME and conducts fifty to seventy physician workshops per year. Barb is the nursing program coordinator and also delivers fifty to seventy programs each year. Janet is the allied health coordinator and works with occupational and physical therapists, speech therapists, rehabilitation specialists, social services professionals, nursing home administrators, pharmacists, and other assorted professionals. Her workshop load is consistent with the others. Outreach is the responsibility of Dave and his staff, who coordinate all details for hospital outreach. Program income is expected to cover both administrative and workshop expenses, and the department is expected to be self-supporting. Currently, income covers all workshop costs but only 50 percent of administrative costs.

The interviews conducted for this case study were intended to gather information about the program planning process at each of the three levels of continuing education administration. One interview was conducted with Greg to look at the goals of the institution and to help define his role from both an academic and an administrative perspective. This interview also provided insight into Greg's level of power and into how Dave uses this power to accomplish his responsibilities. Each of the program coordinators participated in two interviews. The first interview was a discussion based on a fictitious program typical of their particular content area. The second interview focused on a program that each planner had actually planned and implemented. Dave also participated in two interviews. The first provided general information about the structure and role of the Department of Continuing Education, and the second was a discussion about his reactions to information gathered in the three interviews about actual programs with the program coordinators and with Greg. The issues and strategies addressed in the next section are based on a compilation of these interviews.

Continuing Medical Education Issues and Strategies

The CME function at Eastern University exhibits three very distinct levels of power and purpose. Greg, the associate dean, has the power to control and directly influence departments, department heads, and other physicians because he is also a physician and department head. As Dave says, "He is a member of the club, and therefore he handles the difficult political situations." The director of continuing education serves as a buffer for the three program coordinators. His management style allows them to be autonomous, but when difficult situations arise with a faculty member or a department it is directed to him, and he resolves it in conjunction with Greg. The program coordinators are the frontline planners and interact directly with the academic faculty chair on each program within their particular area of responsibility. Their role is to do the initial program assessment, develop and manage the program budget, market the program, and take care of logistics.

Greg sees his role as very heavily weighted toward the physician and responsible for expanding the resources of the College of Medicine beyond the local community. The advent of health care reform has accelerated the efforts of the department to develop programs for physicians in practice and has given it a new direction, which Greg describes as follows:

> The increasing tendency that the medical center has on clinically generated revenue and in reality the increasing dependency that the individual faculty member has for clinical revenue for salary also drives this process. It is well established that when one of our faculty members goes out to an outlying hospital and participates in a CME program, almost invariably we see increased referrals. It is probably our most successful tool in recruiting patients, and it is the easiest foot in the door as far as selling the clinical services that we have here at the institution. Our faculty can write Nobel Prize–winning articles in the most prestigious journals, but the doctor who is practicing in the community will not be aware of that. That doctor will be aware of the faculty member who comes to his or her local hospital and gives a CME program on a new treatment or procedure. So, while it may not be the purest role of CME, it is a very effective marketing tool that the university has for selling clinical services.

Greg sees these referrals as important in keeping the hospital full and the anesthesiologists, surgeons, and nurses working. If they do pick up a few new patients, that money will never show up in the CME budget; yet it is a direct result of the course. With this in mind, Greg looks at the potential that a program has and is willing to underprice it to increase its marketability. The program may lose money this year and maybe the next, but the college is willing to subsidize it because it serves an internal interest.

Another strategy Greg pursues in his role is to serve as an intermediary when a conflict occurs between departments. Many areas in medicine overlap, and ownership of subject material occasionally becomes an issue. These problems are usually brought to Greg's attention by Dave. As an example, someone may give a course on a subject that a subspecialty often gets involved in, such as an internal medicine course on cardiology. One thing that Greg and Dave may do is to meet with the faculty member who is developing the course and suggest that he or she invite faculty from the other area to participate as well. This may double the audience and ensure the success of the program. If there is resistance, usually because of a personality conflict, Greg makes note of his concern that the interests of the department and the college are not being met. This then shifts the burden of responsibility for program success to that faculty member and his or her department and away from the Department of Continuing Education and the program coordinator.

Dave's role as the director of continuing education is one of the most difficult in the organization. He is responsible for defining the goals of the department, developing and meeting the budget, expanding the college's outreach efforts, overseeing the CME accreditation process, and resolving conflicts that occur between his coordinators and faculty or departments that want to deliver programs. He sees his role as being limited by the fact that he does not have academic rank, and he therefore relies on Greg's support and political clout. As he says, "I can push through the administrative details, and I can say this is a rule and you cannot do that, but when things get hot and heavy I send it through the associate dean, and that is his role."

Dave has the responsibility for managing the overall departmental budget, and his operation is expected to be self-supporting. These funds are generated by registration fees from physicians, nurses, and allied health care professionals. As noted, these currently cover program costs but only about 50 percent of administrative costs. This is a source of concern for Dave. He is responsible for ensuring that the department does everything in its power to make programs happen and to serve the needs of the academic departments and faculty of the college, even if that means running a program at a loss. One of his greatest sources of frustration is faculty members who come to the department with unrealistic time lines for programs they want to run. This significantly increases the risk of failure, and the continuing education department still has to absorb the up-front costs of planning and marketing such programs. This also creates conflict in meeting the accreditation requirements of ACCME and has the potential to jeopardize the university's provider status. Another source of frustration is that the department is responsible for coordinating a large number of internal programs (such as grand rounds, which involve eight hundred sessions each year), yet it is not directly compensated for these efforts by the College of Medicine. Dave recognizes the importance of referrals, because patient dollars are the main income stream for the College of Medicine. As he says,

> The primary reason for CME at Eastern University is to generate referral bases. In other words, if we want to establish a base in the Southport area, we do programs and maintain those links. I remember a research article several years ago that looked at the number of follow-up calls after a CME event, and it showed indeed that when you held a program your number of calls increased over a period of time and then decreased; so that if you did not go back in like thirty to ninety days, it would peak and then go down. If you were out of their sight for three months, then all of a sudden they did not think of you. The distance from the medical center is also a factor. Once you get two or three hours away from your institution, your referral base drops off. You get calls and contacts, but they do not refer patients to you. So that kind of sets the pattern and makes a good strong case for doing programs, because people get to know you and associate that with you.

The importance of referrals and the university's dependence on them seems very clear to Greg, the associate dean, and Dave, the director, but when Dave was asked if this was an institutional understanding and a role that the program coordinators also clearly understood and supported, he said:

> I do not think it is in the planner's mind at all. The planners are looking at tying groups together and matching a need with a resource, and that is basically all that they are doing. I do not think they see it as the big picture. Even the faculty, most times, do not see it, or if they do see it they do not recognize its importance. They will say, "Yes, this is important, but if you cannot pay me $500 I will not do it." So you have to tell them that if you do this and get several referrals you are going to make much more than $500, so even they do not see it. I think it is important at the upper levels of the institution—the dean's level. The associate deans and assistant deans understand it, the department chairs sort of—but they have a loyalty more to the faculty, and then all of a sudden you are at the faculty level. Although they may say they understand, they either do not want to participate, or they really do not understand.

The three program coordinators see their roles from another perspective. Each considers herself a risk taker and is willing to run with most new program ideas at least once. They depend on their academic program chairs to know what the currently important and relevant topics are in each content area. They gather information in an initial planning meeting and then develop a program budget based on that discussion. A part of that budget process includes a determination of a minimum number of registrants required for the program to at least break even. This number plays an important role in the program planning process. Each coordinator has an annual programming quota that they are expected to meet. This quota actually amounts to a minimum spread of profit that they are to return, based on their total program mix. This mix is usually a combination of new and repeat programs, which may come from either internal or external sources. All three planners are increasingly aware of this pressure to generate a profit, and this has affected their planning and program selection process. All three planners also look at their role from a customer service perspective, making every effort to meet the needs of the faculty and the department.

Carol is the coordinator responsible for physician CME; she deals with the most politically difficult situations. Much of this is based on the asymmetrical power relationship between her position and physicians. As one of the other coordinators stated, "Physician programming is going to happen no matter what, because that is our primary function—to provide continuing medical education." CME programs are also very price-sensitive, as they often depend on outside support from commercial vendors and pharmaceutical companies. Of all the programs offered by the Department of Continuing Education, those for physicians have the lowest registration fees on average, although physicians have the highest average income. This puts additional financial pressure on,

Carol, because her budget typically includes an estimate of how much the physician or department thinks they can attract from external sources. If this estimate falls short, the Department of Continuing Education assumes the risk and usually absorbs the loss. Carol sometimes plans programs with the goal of increasing referrals, but this is usually based on the expressed interest of a faculty member or the department and not her intent. More often her purpose is to meet the needs of the individual academic chair so that he or she will continue to use the services of the department and possibly refer colleagues to her for other potential programs. One program that she coordinated involved actual live surgery for the participants to observe. Her next goal is to expand this program through the use of distance education technology to participants at other locations, but referrals did not play a cognizant role in her planning process.

She did mention two programs during this past year, one for neurology and the other for orthopedics, that specifically focus on increasing referrals. One of the strategies she used was to process accreditation approval from the American Academy of Family Physicians (AAFP) in order to make the programs more appealing to primary care physicians. She also solicited mailing lists from the AAFP in order to target her promotional mailing. Both of these strategies were implemented with the intent of building relationships between the specialists and the family physicians. Another strategy she has used is to provide complimentary registrations to medical students and physicians who are completing their residencies. This has two potential benefits. First, when these students set up their own practice, they may consider using the medical center for their patients. Second, they may also consider the Department of Continuing Education for their CME needs in the future. Both scenarios are certainly more long-term and high-risk in nature.

Barb is the coordinator for nursing programs. She serves the educational needs of both the internal nursing staff and nurses from the community. Her patient referrals are usually limited to multidisciplinary programs that involve physicians, but this is usually not her first priority in her planning activities. She believes that her program indirectly builds referrals because of improved patient care. If the patients have a good experience during their hospital stay, they may recommend the institution to other family members or friends. She cosponsored a program this past year with a newly formed chapter of the American Association of Neuroscience Nurses (AANN). The chapter provided AANN accreditation and also encouraged its current members to enroll in the program. The association's goal was not only to provide more continuing education to its membership and to meet their professional development needs but also to also try and attract new members to the local chapter. In this case, additional nurses registered for Barb's program, and the AANN received increased promotion and credibility.

Janet coordinates programs for allied health professionals. Her responsibilities are the most varied, and her constituents include paraprofessionals, nurses, and physicians. Her programs are the most difficult to track as far as referrals are concerned. Her area is also the most politically vulnerable, because the College of Medicine does not have any departments within it that are directly related to allied health. Therefore she does not have a direct advocate in Greg. A case in point is an annual sports medicine program she has coordinated for the past several years. The program was originally developed by an orthopedic physician with an interest in sports medicine, with the intent of increasing physician referrals. The program was interdisciplinary and attracted some primary care physicians, physical therapists, trainers, and coaches. It was financially successful, but it never really caught on with physicians. Janet has tried several different marketing approaches. One year she even developed different tracks within the program to address the individual needs of the different groups, but the physician track only drew ten or twelve participants. This past year she asked the Department of Family Medicine to cosponsor the program with the orthopedics department and saw a significant increase in the number of primary care physicians. She felt that the fact that Family Medicine speakers were part of the program may have added credibility and increased the interest among family practitioners. An interesting twist to this program is that the physician who originally developed it retired this past year, and a new head of orthopaedics was named. He has decided to redesign the program and direct it to a physician-only audience. This means that the audience of allied health professionals have lost an important source of continuing professional education. When asked if the program would be offered next year, Janet said, "Probably not, at least not in its current format and probably not through the medical center." The primary reason is that the new head of orthopedics is very supportive of continuing education and sees it as an important source of referral revenue. Janet believes that the department has the power to make the final decision and says, "Physician programming is the first priority here, and it pays the bills and keeps us our jobs. Plus, even if that was not the case, if I did a program for coaches I would probably want a physician to come and speak—so why would I cut my throat?"

Learning from Practice

The interviews with the associate dean and the director of continuing education clearly support the importance of referrals as part of the CME planning process. This certainly satisfies a real interest of the institution, by providing needed revenue to support the clinical services offered by the College of Medicine and by helping cover the salaries of faculty members. It also serves an expressed interest, by providing needed continuing professional education opportunities for physicians and other health care providers in the community and by building ongoing relationships that potentially benefit the patient. Programs developed to build referrals also have the potential to improve the skills of primary care physicians and to provide them with other resources and specialists, thereby enhancing the quality of patient care.

A major concern that this case study demonstrates is that the importance of referrals has not been clearly expressed to the program coordinators, department heads, and faculty at Eastern University. Because of this lack of communication, the administration of the institution seems to have a different interest from the faculty and staff. This certainly has the potential to affect the program planning and budgetary process and to create an ethical conflict for the coordinators, because they may have to decide between the real interest of generating referrals and the expressed interest of running the program on a cost-recovery basis. The message they have received from Dave is that they are to generate a certain amount of revenue with their programs. Greg's message is that the college is willing to run these programs at a loss if it keeps professionals working and beds full. The problem is that referrals generated as a result of programs are not being tracked, and therefore the Department of Continuing Education receives no credit for them. The coordinator may decide to cancel a program without this information—and then fail to meet the interests of the college, the academic chair, and the participants. If these numbers were tracked, they could also be shared with faculty and department heads and used to encourage them to expand the number of programs they offer. Taking it a step further, the program coordinators could more specifically define their target market by focusing on primary care physicians that practice close enough to the medical center to refer patients, and programs could be repeated often enough for local hospitals to consider Eastern University their primary CME provider and then, perhaps, become a first choice for patient referrals. Finally, the program coordinators could consider cosponsoring more programs with professional associations like the AAFP to entice more family physicians to attend the department's programs and meet the university's needs.

Physicians may find the idea of focusing a program on generating referrals ethically difficult to support. Most physicians have as their primary goal to improve the quality of patient care, and this is supported by the majority of CME program planning models. Greg somewhat hinted at this when he said that generating referrals may not be CME's purest role. It may also create conflict for the coordinators, because their focus is on customer service and meeting the interests of the academic chair. This is due, in part, to the major emphasis on total quality management and continuous improvement that most major institutions have experienced in the past several years. The planners do not think of their role in terms of negotiating levels of power and serving real interests. Instead, they are thinking of how they can satisfy the expressed needs of academic chairs and build long-term relationships with them.

Finally, it would seem that the College of Medicine needs to reexamine the role it wants the Department of Continuing Education to play and clearly communicate this to its members. If the college truly wants the department to be self-supporting, it may want to reconsider who assumes all of the financial risk if a program does not run or the department does not actually receive as much external support from outside vendors as projected. This might require the department and the college to share the risk. As managed care continues to grow and resources become more scarce, the role of the program planner as risk taker may dwindle. The college also needs to address the issue of the number of internal services the department provides and give it some type of financial recognition for it. This might include a permanent subsidy for CME or guaranteed support through registrations for all of the programs the department offers.

From a program planning model perspective, we need to continue to bridge the gap between prescriptive theory and what program planners are actually doing to serve the needs of learners and the interests of their institution. This is only one example of an area that has not been addressed in the literature, but it is an especially important consideration to major medical institutions and providers of CME.

References

Brown, C. R., and Uhl, H.S.M. "Mandatory Continuing Education: Sense or Nonsense?" *Journal of the American Medical Association,* 1970, *213,* 1660–1668.

Cervero, R. M. "Collaboration in University Continuing Professional Education." In H. Beder (ed.), *Realizing the Potential of Interorganizational Cooperation.* New Directions for Continuing Education, no. 23. San Francisco: Jossey-Bass, 1984.

Cervero, R. M., and Wilson, A. L. *Planning Responsibly for Adult Education: A Guide to Negotiating Power and Interests.* San Francisco: Jossey-Bass, 1994.

Mazmanian, P. E. "A Decision-Making Approach to Needs Assessment and Objective Setting in Continuing Medical Education." *Adult Education,* 1980, *31* (1), 3–17.

Moore, D. E. "Evolving Approaches to Continuing Medical Education: Efforts to Enhance the Impact on Patient Care." In J. S. Green, S. J. Grosswald, E. Suter, and D. B. Walthall III (eds.), *Continuing Education for the Health Professions: Developing, Managing, and Evaluating Programs for Maximum Impact on Patient Care.* San Francisco: Jossey-Bass, 1984.

Sork, T. J. "Theoretical Foundations of Educational Program Planning." *Journal of Continuing Education in the Health Professions,* 1990, *10* (1), 73–83.

Walsh, P. L. "Planning and Developing Programs Systematically." In J. S. Green, S. J. Grosswald, E. Suter, and D. B. Walthall III (eds.), *Continuing Education for the Health Professions: Developing, Managing, and Evaluating Programs for Maximum Impact on Patient Care.* San Francisco: Jossey-Bass, 1984.

ROGER G. MACLEAN is continuing and distance education coordinator for the College of the Liberal Arts, The Pennsylvania State University. Previously he worked in the pharmaceutical industry and in sales and marketing, and planned continuing medical education programs.

An analysis of the social dynamics of negotiating curriculum development for an independent study distance education program in higher education is presented.

Leveling the Playing Field for Planning University-Based Distance Education

Pamela B. Kleiber

The politics of planning for distance education in a university setting is influenced by the marginal position of distance education in higher education. The attitude of on-campus faculty and administrators that distance education is inferior is well documented in the distance education literature (Dunning, Van Kekerix, and Zaborowski, 1993; Verduin and Clark, 1991; Keegan, 1990). These people must be involved in planning and implementing distance education; therefore, as Verduin and Clark (1991) point out, "Unless their attitudes and perceptions change, it is unlikely that distance education will be accepted and utilized as a mainstream method of delivery in American adult and higher education" (p. 87).

As the oldest form of distance education, correspondence study (recently renamed independent study) has long dealt with the issue of perceived quality. Even though research has demonstrated that the learning outcomes from correspondence study are equal to or better than those of face-to-face instruction, image problems remain (Pittman, 1991). In most, if not all, instances, distance education efforts in universities require the approval of the academic department where the course or program originates. Thus, the perceptions of department administrators concerning the effectiveness of distance education are critical to program development. "The research on distance higher and adult education, and the findings and conclusions based on it, may be useful to people engaged in the current dialogue concerning the effectiveness and quality of this innovative means of delivery in education" (Verduin and Clark, 1991, p. 87).

Planners often face asymmetrical power relationships in developing educational programs (Cervero and Wilson, 1994). In the case of independent study and most other distance education programs, the imbalance results from the need to gain approval from the academic departments. Considerable discussion and negotiation are necessary to establish broad-based working relationships among faculty, academic departments, and independent study programs. Planners who do not consider the politics of this situation are "ignoring the opportunities and dangers of an organizational setting [which] is like walking across a busy intersection with one's eyes closed" (Forester, 1989, p. 7). Academic departments that have had positive experiences with independent study programs may continue to support them with little or no prodding, but additional strategies may be required to level the playing field with departments that have no previous experience with independent study.

To avoid blindly walking across a busy intersection, I use the theoretical framework of Cervero and Wilson (1994) in this chapter to analyze curriculum development practices for independent study in higher education. The chapter considers my role as a planner of an independent study program for undergraduate academic credit. I discuss three specific negotiation strategies I have used with departments that had no prior experience with independent study. This analysis seeks to understand how interests have been negotiated in developing the curriculum for the University System of Georgia Independent Study (USGIS) program.

Organizational Context

Independent study programs exist in colleges and universities throughout the country to provide alternative access to an undergraduate education, freeing students from the restrictions imposed by geography and time. The USGIS program provides an example of a fairly common arrangement. The curriculum itself is developed through the collaborative interactions of people in the service and academic sectors of the university. The University of Georgia is a land-grant institution with a mission of providing education to the people of the state. As with other states that have invested heavily in the distance education movement, such as Wisconsin, Minnesota, and Iowa, Georgia has a significant rural population for whom geography is a barrier to participation. Providing undergraduate college courses to these persons is the primary role of USGIS. Five participating institutions, Georgia College, Georgia Southern University, North Georgia College, University of Georgia, and Valdosta State University, offer courses through USGIS. The program is administered through the University of Georgia Center for Continuing Education.

There are various stakeholders associated with USGIS. As Cervero and Wilson (1994) explain, "educational programs are constructed by people with particular interests who have relations of power with each other" (p. 29). The public; the students, faculty, and academic departments of the participating institutions; and the USGIS program all have particular interests, and discernible power relationships exist among them. The balance of power is tipped toward the academic departments. The USGIS program, the faculty members, and the academic departments all represent the students', the public's, and their own interests, but they can differ in how they interpret their various responsibilities. The context for developing each course varies considerably, but some patterns for considering political boundedness are apparent (Cervero and Wilson, 1994). Faculty, academic departments, and the USGIS coordinator for curriculum development (or the appropriate department head) enter into discussions (initiated by any of the three parties) to determine if a specific course will be offered through USGIS and, if so, what instructional design and technology will be used (Van Kekerix and Andrews, 1991) and who will develop and teach it.

In general, the primary interest shared by most of the stakeholders is to provide educational opportunities for students who, for whatever reason, cannot attend the course on campus at the scheduled time. In some departments, the first concern may be to help regular students meet their graduation requirements on time. In other departments, a primary concern may be to serve students who are unable to be "regular" students. When such service is not an interest of a department or of any of its faculty members, a USGIS course is seldom developed. USGIS shares an interest in providing access to undergraduate academic credit for all academic areas. A related concern may be that of the faculty member who is not compensated for instructing independent study students. USGIS offers a way to compensate faculty for instructing these students. A secondary interest that may or may not be shared by all parties is the desire to participate in the distance education arena and experiment with various technologies for use in course design and delivery. USGIS can provide technical assistance and financial compensation for faculty interested in developing innovative instructional materials and strategies. A third interest is the maintenance or enhancement of the reputation of both the academic department and of USGIS. It is in the interest of both the academic department and USGIS to offer a rigorous distance learning program. Raising the level of academic participation is also an interest of USGIS: the greater the level of faculty participation in USGIS, the broader the support for the program across the system.

Strategies for Negotiating Interests

It is very important to note that the curriculum development process is highly structured at the institutional level. In order to award academic credit from the university, a USGIS course must be comparable to its on-campus counterpart. Therefore, the course must contain essentially the same content, and in many cases it is taught by an instructor who has taught the course at the originating institution. Courses that are not being taught at a participating institution cannot be developed for USGIS. Decisions to add or drop a course from the curriculum are at the discretion of the academic departments, with input from faculty and USGIS. While this is a highly structured arrangement, there are a number of aspects to negotiate. The public and the students do not participate in planning, except to the extent that their interests are represented by the planners. Nevertheless, in keeping with Cervero and Wilson (1994), I see my role in planning as representing the interests of the public, the students, and the program itself when I negotiate with academic departments and faculty to offer courses through USGIS. In a recent national survey conducted by the Social and Economic Research Center at Washington State University, 77 percent of the respondents said that universities should develop more distance education ("National Survey Reveals . . . ," 1995).

Use of Technical Data. In order to plan in a systematic and responsible fashion, USGIS has collected technical data for use in evaluating courses, determining priorities for curriculum development, gauging faculty and student access to and interest in technology, and benchmarking our own program against other independent study programs in university settings. Specifically, a curriculum assessment, an institutional E-mail survey, a faculty E-mail survey, a student technology survey, and individual student course evaluations are used as sources of technical data. During my initial contacts with academic department heads and faculty, I usually refer to this data to inform them about the program and to answer any concerns. After some time now in the position, I can anticipate what information may be particularly salient. In the process, I negotiate for public and student access to academic credit courses for increased USGIS offerings. I am most likely to use these data to get to the negotiating table.

Structured Course Study Guides. Once I arrive at the table, more specific questions arise as to how the course will be developed and taught through USGIS. We have developed components for USGIS course study guides, based on National University Continuing Education Association (NUCEA) standards for independent study, which include specific assignments, learning objectives, discussion sections, and guidelines for the use of media. Faculty are compensated on a per-lesson-graded basis, which requires feedback to students on at least nine occasions and a final examination. In addition, we have a very well developed course evaluation system that is similar to the on-campus course evaluation process. USGIS sends course evaluation reports to course instructors and the academic department heads on a quarterly basis.

Feedback is used to make changes in the course as appropriate. Most faculty members and department heads appreciate this process as a quality control measure, and we try to accommodate particular course needs and individual teaching styles. We have also developed an independent study author's manual, which is given to each course developer in order to assist with course development. The editorial and production manager and I, as coordinator for curriculum development, consult with faculty during the course development process. Technical assistants also work with faculty for courses that require media development. Out of more than one hundred course developments and revisions, only once has a faculty member found the format too constraining. In most cases, the course development and revision process has helped USGIS gain acceptance and approval.

Formal Agreements. Once we have reached a general understanding among the faculty member, academic department head, and USGIS, we issue a formal, written agreement that will govern the course's development or revision as well as its instruction. If media are to be developed, we negotiate a specific agreement outlining the responsibilities and expectations of all parties. These interdepartmental agreements are signed by the faculty member, her or his academic department head, the coordinator for curriculum development, and USGIS. We have found that this process improves our ability to have all parties follow through on the agreement. The formal agreement process provides the academic department with written documentation. It also protects the faculty member, who will be investing his or her time with the expectation of being compensated for course development and instructional services rendered. This process also protects the interests of USGIS related to planning and capital fund expenditure.

How Interests Are Negotiated

The following vignettes document how technical data, structured course development, and formalized agreements are used to negotiate interests in developing courses for USGIS.

Developing Laboratory Science Courses. When I was hired as coordinator for curriculum development and was completely new to USGIS, I learned that most course offerings were in the humanities, while science courses could be considered for development with the use of new technologies. Humanities courses have lent themselves more readily to the traditional correspondence course format than have science courses. More recently, the emphasis has been on using media and learning centers for independent study science courses. A new distance education classroom and new technical expertise at the University of Georgia Center for Continuing Education can now be used to support courses requiring media enhancements. I realized that offering such courses would improve service to students and enhance the reputation of USGIS.

I was given the name of a part-time instructor of a basic science course for nonmajors as someone to talk with about developing USGIS science offerings. I called her and was quite impressed with her interest and experience and with the student evaluations from her course. We discussed how various technologies would be useful in teaching the course at a distance. She was clearly interested in experimenting with distance teaching. We discussed the way USGIS courses are structured, with feedback to students, and how laboratory exercises could be videotaped. Another major consideration was how laboratory kits could be packaged and disseminated to students. After this conversation, the instructor approached her department; afterward, she was discouraged about the prospect. Since I had not been part of the discussion, I suggested that I could telephone the department chair to discuss the department's interest in developing the course for USGIS and address any of the department's concerns. When we want to develop a particular course for USGIS and we know of an instructor who is well regarded, we often negotiate directly with the instructor, who in turn negotiates with his or her department. This approach works in many instances, but it was not sufficient in this case.

The department chair said that a number of questions had arisen during her discussion with the instructor and that she would be happy to discuss them with me. We talked for more than an hour on the phone about how USGIS works; the curriculum assessment, which had identified the course as one in high demand; the challenges of teaching a laboratory component of a science course at a distance, and how we might address them; and the demographics and other characteristics of our students. I used a great deal of technical data in these early conversations in order to make a case for offering this course through an alternative format, which I considered to be in the interests of the public and the students as well as USGIS. If the number of lessons, feedback loops, and proctored examinations had to be continually negotiated, we would be faced with either more extensive negotiations or the possibility of offering substandard courses. The structure of an independent study course compromises instructor spontaneity, but this is seen as a trade-off in ensuring that certain standards are met. We make this choice and then try to accommodate individual teaching styles during course development.

The department head asked me to put the essence of our conversation into a detailed memorandum, including our discussion of a video-based approach to the course, and send it to her so she could discuss it with her faculty. She communicated reserved interest. She was apparently interested in various departmental concerns, the potential of distance education, and preserving the reputation of the department. The videotape added a new dimension of concern for the reputation of the department, since "if you make a mistake in a lecture, you can correct it in the next lecture. However, video is an unforgiving medium." Therefore, if the department decided to go forward with this course, they wanted to take every precaution in developing a flawless course that would put the department's best talent forward.

In a few weeks, I followed up with a phone call to the department head and asked if she had spoken with the faculty. She said she had and then asked if I would be willing to meet with the department's curriculum committee about the ideas. We arranged to meet one week later. When I met with this committee of four faculty members plus the department head, I used some of the technical data we had collected to answer a number of questions they had. Information from our student technology survey was used to establish our interest in utilizing technology and students' interest in having technological course components.

One of the structures we work within is that USGIS courses are taught by faculty members approved by the academic department where they originate. I explained that we would not and could not offer a course without their approval. This policy often has the effect of reassuring the department head that the department's control of the curriculum will not be relinquished. Usually this is very effective in establishing dialogue. In fact, this was a very important issue for this particular department. If they were going to be involved in producing a video-based version of the course, they wanted the very best instructor to teach it. After we were all in agreement over this, we discussed who might teach it.

There was some disagreement among the faculty as to whether it was a good idea to try to teach this course at a distance. One faculty member asked if USGIS would offer the course through another participating institution if this department decided not to offer it. I replied that we wanted to offer a quality laboratory science course, and if they declined and we were able to accomplish that with another participating institution, then we would. The fact that there are five participating institutions improves our ability to develop a course, since we are not dependent upon only one for cooperation. The discussion then moved back to who would teach the course. Again I said that the department would need to make a recommendation. At this point, discussion moved to the state of science teaching at the undergraduate level. The group explained that the department was considering hiring a new faculty member whose scholarship concentrates on the teaching of science. How this course would be taught was very important to this group of faculty, and some were very open in noting that they did not know if they had an individual who would be ready to tackle a distance education version of it.

Further consideration of who would teach the course brought up the issue of financial compensation. They considered the compensation I could offer for course and media development to be considerably inadequate, given the work it would take. I explained that multimedia development for independent study is new and that we would be further examining issues related to compensation. I later used information from this discussion to negotiate with upper administration to increase the amount of compensation for faculty engaged in course development. The curriculum committee suggested that I might meet faculty who would be interviewing for the position and discuss the independent study opportunity, and that each candidate might visit the new distance education classroom in the University of Georgia Center for Continuing Education.

It is now time for me to reconnect with them and find out where they are in the process of considering who might teach a distance education laboratory science course and to let them know that we have successfully increased the amount of compensation we can offer faculty for course and related technology development. Negotiations for course development through USGIS often take a long time. The most important thing is to keep the door open and the prospects on the table. Ultimately, USGIS wants to add such courses, but it sometimes takes time to get everyone on board.

Refining the USGIS Language Sequence. USGIS has had a four-part language sequence in its curriculum for many years. Students evaluate the course positively; however, the course focuses on the written rather than the spoken word. The instructor does not address diversity among cultures in which this language is spoken. Our environmental scanning efforts have indicated that courses that use technology to teach languages and give attention to diversity are popular as well as pedagogically sound. While the student does use language tapes in the current course, there are no mechanisms for offering feedback on how students are speaking the language. Other USGIS courses that use audiotapes or videotapes do have feedback mechanisms.

We spoke with the instructor of the language sequence about incorporating these elements into a revision of the course. He was not interested in changing the course, however, and referred us to the positive evaluations of the course. From our perspective, though, there is a place for another version of this language course that emphasizes cultural diversity and the spoken word. Our curriculum assessment identified this language sequence as being in high demand across the system. In fact, the course at the originating institution limits enrollment for pedagogical reasons. Our environmental scanning data indicated that there is also a need for emphasizing cultural diversity as well as the ability to actually speak another language. I have personally had students come to my office and call me on the telephone who would like to take a language course through USGIS while traveling abroad. A course taught differently would accommodate their needs better. After not reaching an agreement with the current instructor, I discussed this interest with a faculty member who knew of an instructor who might be interested.

This networking was useful. The language instructor approached me about the possibility of redeveloping the language sequence to emphasize the diversity of this language and the cultures in which it is spoken. Since I was very interested and he seemed to share the same pedagogical interests, we set up a meeting. During the meeting, he asked me very frankly if students enrolled in the independent study course to avoid speaking the language. Of course, it is difficult to determine the answer to this question absolutely, but I told him that our student enrollment data indicate that scheduling and distance problems are the primary reason students enroll in USGIS. It is the better student who successfully completes and earns academic credit through USGIS. I added that we have students who want to learn to speak the language as well as understand the written and spoken word, sometimes in the context of a particular culture. It is with these students in mind that we were considering developing another approach. I also shared the results of the technology survey, which indicated that a significant number of students prefer a technological component, that the vast majority have access to audiotape and videotape players, and that a majority also have access to computers.

This instructor has had considerable experience with the cultures that speak this language. He is very interested in the pedagogy of second language acquisition, including instructional strategies that use technology. In fact, his department has wanted to develop new technology-based instructional materials for the classroom. Since the instructor will receive a personal copy of any new instructional media produced specifically for the USGIS course, the department will also have access to it for on-campus use. This instructor was interested in the opportunity to develop course materials using the technology and expertise available at the Center for Continuing Education. He suggested that he meet with his department head to determine the department's interest in supporting the project. I received a call a few days later saying that the department head had already given his full support. In addition, this instructor had secured volunteer support within the department from other faculty and graduate students to work on the media development using vignettes with native speakers. I have initiated the paperwork necessary to have the faculty member approved and the course added to our inventory. Agreements for course preparation of a four-course sequence, with accompanying media development, will follow. The formal agreement will ensure the instructor and the department that USGIS will follow through on course development by certain dates. It also ensures USGIS that the sequence of courses will be available for registration within one calendar year.

Learning from Practice

USGIS must deal with many structural constraints in developing curriculum, but there is also a great deal of opportunity for negotiating various interests. Institutional interests—in particular, the reputation of academic departments and the comparability of USGIS courses with regular classes—are protected by the structure of the system. The asymmetrical power relationships favor the academic departments, but USGIS can gain power through negotiation. Within the bureaucratic constraints imposed by the system, faculty, administrators, and USGIS planners have a great deal of room for discussion and decision making concerning whether or not a course should be adapted for independent study, who will teach it, and how it will be designed.

The design of the data collection process allows planners to consider where the opportunities are and whose interests we need to represent and how. We have found technical data helpful in determining where and how to initiate these discussions as well as in representing various interests. Faculty and administrators have been very responsive to the fact that we have collected the data and to the findings themselves. But this information is shared in an informal way most of the time. The only formal sharing of data has been in quarterly reports of student evaluations.

We have also found that there is a great deal more room for negotiation with some departments than with others in terms of the courses that can be developed, by whom, and in what way. We use different data in different ways with different departments. Other programs might very well collect different data than those that we have found useful. Indeed, we may collect different data ourselves for future planning. Although USGIS course study guides have standard components, this practice has served to enhance our ability to negotiate. It offers rigor and provides some evidence that what is being taught and learned in USGIS courses is comparable to what on-campus courses provide. Our course development process does restrict individualized instruction, which is a concern we try to address in specific ways with individual instructors as best we can. The basic standards for accreditation and the requirements of the participating colleges and universities are nonnegotiable on the day-to-day operational level. However, changes in demographics, technology, and the public's expectations of higher education may all contribute to our ability to renegotiate current determinants such as limits on the number of hours of independent study a student can apply toward earning a degree.

For a century, correspondence courses have been the most enduring form of distance education. New technologies promise to transform the way we think of independent study, with students engaging in independent learning on the Internet through newsgroups, listservs, and E-mail dialogue with faculty and fellow students. Independent study will affect and be affected by other forms of distance education as well. These changes will force us all to question whether face-to-face education should continue as the "gold standard" of higher education.

References

Cervero, R. M., and Wilson, A. L. *Planning Responsibly for Adult Education: A Guide to Negotiating Power and Interests.* San Francisco: Jossey-Bass, 1994.

Duning, B. S., Van Kekerix, M. J., and Zaborowski, L. M. *Reaching Learners Through Telecommunications: Management and Leadership Strategies for Higher Education.* San Francisco: Jossey-Bass, 1993.

Forester, J. *Planning in the Face of Power.* Berkeley: University of California Press, 1989.

Keegan, D. *Foundations of Distance Education.* (2nd ed.) New York: Routledge & Kegan Paul, 1990.

"National Survey Reveals Strong Public Support for Expanded University C. E. Services." *NUCEA News,* 1995, *11* (9), 1, 8.

Pittman, V. "Academic Credibility and the 'Image Problem': The Quality Issue in Collegiate Independent Study." In B. L. Watkins and S. J. Wright (eds.), *The Foundations of American Distance Education: A Century of Collegiate Correspondence Study.* Dubuque, Iowa: Kendall-Hunt, 1991.

Van Kekerix, M., and Andrews, J. "Electronic Media and Independent Study." In B. L. Watkins and S. J. Wright (eds.), *The Foundations of American Distance Education: A Century of Collegiate Correspondence Study.* Dubuque, Iowa: Kendall-Hunt, 1991.

Verduin, J. R., Jr., and Clark, T. A. *Distance Education: The Foundations of Effective Practice.* San Francisco: Jossey-Bass, 1991.

PAMELA B. KLEIBER is coordinator of curriculum development for the Georgia University System independent study program at the University of Georgia Center for Continuing Education, Athens, Georgia.

This case study of a women's collective in Canada provides a context for discussing conflicting interests and ethical dilemmas as planners work in community-based programs.

Collective Action by Women in Community-Based Program Planning

Sue M. Scott, Margo Schmitt-Boshnick

Program planners in all educational organizations and situations are responsible for carrying out the various steps of program planning and for understanding the context and politics involved. The situation for planners in community-based contexts differs from those who plan institutional programs, however, in that the direction comes from the learners themselves. Grassroots organizations are usually flat in structure, with few administrative personnel. The stakeholder population consists of board members, volunteers, and participants as well as government programmers, funders, and policy makers. Program planners must work with all interests, keeping in mind that the learner comes first. Operating with a guiding principle of participation as the foundation for program planning makes it challenging for the program planner as ethical dilemmas emerge in the negotiation process. This chapter examines the intentionality of the program planner and the ethical dilemmas encountered as she works through the negotiation process with a community-based, grassroots organization.

Community-Based Education: Models, Processes, and Programs

An examination of the literature on community-based or grassroots education reveals numerous models, processes, and programs. Because of the emancipatory and process-based nature of this type of education, a great deal has been written about the involvement of the community or organization in determining its own future. However, much of this literature does not address program planning specifically, nor does it provide a detailed analysis of the role of the planner or educator. For example, Hamilton and Cunningham (1989) provide an extensive overview of community development and popular education. They draw on a number of theorists to flesh out their discussion. Although their writing provides a conceptual direction for understanding the educational experience in the community, including program planning, it does not discuss what planners do.

This lack of analysis of what really happens in community-based program planning is evident in other writings as well. Heaney and Horton (1990) also address community-based or grassroots education and social change. Although they do not discuss program planning specifically, Heaney and Horton draw upon Freire's notion (1970) of conscientization to discuss the educational experience and the role of the educator in facilitating critical reflection. To a large extent, the context and politics that affect program planning are not illuminated in their discussion, but they are embedded in the examples they provide of community organizing in tenement housing developments. Lovett (1982, 1988) and Clarke, Kilmurray, and Lovett (1983) also provide some case examples of community-based adult education, particularly within working-class communities; but again, they fit them into particular models or processes. Like Heaney and Horton (1990), they neglect the specifics of program planning within the educational environment. Their discussions of the educational planner's role are quite general.

The literature on education within women's grassroots organizations is another avenue for exploring the community-based context. Thompson (1988) provides an overview of the types of emancipatory education within the women's movement. Hart (1990) expands this discussion and looks at the specifics of the consciousness-raising experience. She also suggests some principles for the educator in facilitating this type of educational experience. Her discussion on the operation of consensus within collectives (Hart, 1985) provides some insight into how program planning occurs within a grassroots context.

It is clear that "adults acting collectively are the most able agents for community problem solving and change" (Hamilton and Cunningham, 1989, p. 440). This literature on workers', community, and grassroots education talks about the need for emancipation, but it does not go into the specifics or consequences of actually putting strategies to work. Cervero and Wilson (1994) have contributed to an understanding of the process in planning that gets closer to these consequences. They begin to move beyond the models and examine the issues and consequences of actual planning activities. They use interests, power relationships, and negotiation as heuristics for examining the politics and context of program planning. The case study that follows extends this theoretical framework into the community-based context. Community programmers usually use Freire's planning model (1970). Like those mentioned above, however, this model does not explain how negotiation occurs in a collective, nor does it highlight the dilemmas that the leaders of a collective encounter when attempting to practice democracy in a community. The research reported here addresses these problems. Specifically, it seeks to illuminate processes that are very important in contemporary society: relationship building, listening effectively, critiquing power structures, and acting in concert on shared goals.

The Candora Context

Candora is a nonprofit organization that was originally established by the city of Edmonton's Department of Family and Community Services and as part of the consumer education project of Grant MacEwan Community College. It is run on a community development model that emphasizes community residents' determining their own future rather than deferring to outside experts. Accordingly, residents are hired to work as community facilitators. This provides them with opportunities for personal as well as community development. Although there is a coordinator for the Candora project, the programs and services it offers are primarily determined by the women of Candora themselves.

The name "Candora" stands for "Can Do in Rundle and Abbotsfield," which are two areas in the northeast quadrant of Edmonton, Alberta. These areas were built in the 1970s, during boom years in Alberta, and were intended as low-income housing. Although the city had originally provided funding for the housing complexes, this eventually ceased with dwindling municipal budgets. The developers were not willing to put additional funds into maintaining the complexes, and eventually they fell into disarray. Their decreased value makes them affordable to the working poor and to those on social assistance. As these people have not given voice to the complexes' deteriorating conditions in any organized manner, conditions have continued to decline.

Single-parent families, primarily headed by women, make up a large portion of these communities. Many of these women are isolated, without family or friends in the area, and thus have a low commitment to the community. Candora provides a space for these people to come together, meet people, and identify and take action on some of the problems they are experiencing, such as unemployment, poverty, family violence, and parenting and child care concerns. The community is also home to a diverse group of immigrants, and Candora provides them with a place to address their language and settlement concerns in a collective manner.

Candora is based in the Abbotsfield Mall and is open four days per week. The programs and the staff are funded through Alberta Social Services, the city of Edmonton's Department of Community and Family Services, and various private foundations. The staff consists of a coordinator, the coordinator of the Building a Business Towards Self-Employment program, three outreach workers, an administrative and financial coordinator, and a child care worker. Given the nature of Candora, the board of directors serves mostly as a support. The Personal and Community Enrichment Program, which provides most of the base funding, is designed to give those who have been out of the work force for a long time a preliminary introduction to searching for work.

Participants are involved in a weekly "life choices" program and also work two and a half hours per week at Candora. This is a year-long program, although individuals can leave the program once they feel they are ready for either a more advanced or traditional preemployment program or for employment. Other programs sponsored by Candora include native crafts, sewing, cooking, parenting, a Spanish support group, and collective kitchens.

Principles of Candora. The organization is guided by a set of foundational principles that revolve around honoring women. The women are caught in dependent relationships; that is, they are dependent on men for support, on welfare for money, and on the community for sustenance. Acknowledging this dependency, the women in Candora practice taking control of their lives through taking action in the community. They also use dialogue to critique the structures and social mores of society and of those systems that promote their dependency. Thus, one of Candora's main principles is the notion of participation. As a former coordinator states, "We do not negotiate *for* the women; we negotiate *with* them. It seems to be a hard thing [for outsiders] to understand." Furthermore, "this kind of educational approach works from the belief that the experts are those people who live the issues and the learning needs to be based on that lived reality" (Candora, 1994).

Another principle is that it takes time to change the habits, actions, and internal beliefs of women who have recently come out of isolation. Candora advocates a holistic approach and spurns the prescriptive nature of programs that governments attempt to force them into, as one former coordinator explains:

> Women who have historically not had an employment history and had many barriers to inclusion—to expect them to take part in a three-month program which does not honor their role as mothers, where they are regarded as only caregivers to their children and where they are not honored with the time needed to work through stuff in their lives, [it simply won't work]. If you are to make a shift to work, then it's a shift in balance. That shift has to occur slowly. It has to happen with a whole lot more support. . . . You just force people into a mold, and there's not long-term sustained change. You have to have time to make these shifts.

Giving voice is another important principle within Candora. Many of the women have never really been listened to by their families or by the people who work for the government-funded agencies and programs that affect their lives. Because of this they feel that they have no control over their lives or the power to change things. By voicing and taking action on their concerns, they begin to build confidence in their own abilities to take control. Their personal power is affected as well as their collective power (that is, what they can do within the community to improve things for everyone). This complements the community development principle—that the people in the community determine its future—on which Candora is based.

The principle of equality follows from the principle of giving voice to one's concerns. In Candora all the women have an equal opportunity to guide the direction of the organization. This is especially important within a multicultural situation, where an ethos of respect and tolerance is essential. Equality is also promoted by the nonhierarchical organizational structure. The paid staff must work *with* the women of Candora and the people within the community, not *for* them. They must be present for the women, rather than for the external stakeholders or the activities themselves.

Interests and Power Relationships. The women of Candora bring a variety of interests to the table in program planning. Some are interested in learning instrumental skills, such as economical ways of feeding and clothing their families. Others are in need of companionship and need a community to belong to. They need a place to escape to, to reflect upon the issues that loom large in their lives. As they begin to talk about their reasons for coming to Candora, they often find that others are in similar situations. They begin to discuss ways of overcoming some of the difficulties they face, and soon their private interests became public ones. This is how they determine the type of programs they need; it is also how they develop a sense of power. As marginalized people, their individual interests are overwhelmed by their dependency. Collectively, their interests represent a much more powerful base, and thus they cannot be taken for granted or dismissed readily.

The paid staff, especially the coordinator, come to the table with philosophical and altruistic interests. The coordinator is concerned about being able to put a philosophy of participatory education into practice as well as to promote social justice and social change. A concern for marginalized people complements a need for finding alternative ways of working. The coordinator must work with the others to facilitate the process, rather than dictating it. Although the coordinator is part of the collective, she must acknowledge that her position implies a certain degree of hierarchy within the organization and that it carries a degree of power. It is necessary for her to use her position to facilitate the development of personal and collective power for the women. She must be constantly aware of her motives, so as not to pursue only her own agenda but to maintain a full understanding of the needs and issues of the women in the collective. In the eyes of the collective's funders, she holds more power than any of the other women. She needs to use this perception for the purposes of the group.

Stakeholders outside the organization also have interests that are important in planning its programs. In contrast to the alternative nature of the organization, the external stakeholders are more mainstream in their view of the world. Government funders, in particular, have interests that reflect current priorities of program efficiency and standardization. Funders are the stakeholders with the greatest power. The philosophy of "people before programs" does not fit well with funders geared to increasingly prescriptive programming. It makes it difficult to balance both sides of the coin, as the current coordinator states: "The one thing that is becoming increasingly apparent to me is that the way we operate already has come in conflict with the expectations of funders because we try to be responsive, fluid, flexible. Yet we are hearing strategic planning, long-term goals, accountability, and those things may or may not be compatible. It puts us in some kind of jeopardy, because how can we honor women and children and what is important in the area if we are being dictated to by people who say you will use your money in a certain way?" These power dynamics weigh heavily on the planning process, and Candora must work to maintain its guiding principles. Internal power relationships also affect the process and are dealt with by means of the principles of giving voice to concerns and equality. The following section outlines some of the ways that Candora, particularly the coordinator, takes into account all these interests and power relationships in the planning process.

Ethical Dilemmas in Negotiation

Despite the recent climate shift to right-wing neoconservatism, Candora has continued to provide excellent programming for women. Funders and programmers who have experienced the kind of thinking the Candora women use have come to respect the long-term relationships and commitments required for these women to become involved. The coordinator is an important person in the dynamics of facilitating the organization. She does not see herself as a detached professional who must view the women she serves objectively. Rather, she is immersed in the group and has a vested interest in the success of its programs, the livelihood of the organization, and the well-being of the women themselves. As the program planner, she is both a part of the collective and its spokesperson. That is, she talks to outside stakeholders and plans strategies for getting the two sides together. She never acts alone, and she works to have women in the collective involved in all aspects of negotiation. As with all other aspects of Candora, program planning is based on the principles of the organization. Below are three examples that illustrate the intentions of the coordinator, the ethical dilemmas she faces, the strategies the women of Candora use, and the consequences of their actions.

The coordinator plans and executes programs with the women in the collective. This means ensuring that all parties are aware of the interests at the table as programs are being planned. Thus, when a government representative or funder shows an interest in Candora, he or she is invited to a meeting with the group. As many as twenty to thirty women are present at these meetings. The guests are encouraged to sit anywhere among the women, not at the head of the table. The intention is to neutralize the power of the funders on Candora's turf and to give them a feel for the place. Rarely do government funders actually see people who benefit from the programs they fund. By including the women of Candora in this situation, the funders have less opportunity to dismiss their reality. In Candora the women, as opposed to the coordinator, begin the relationship-building process with funders. It is a practice that they are learning both in the group and in their personal lives. It involves discussing interests and disclosing the details of lives in turmoil in a climate of trust. Guests are simply folded into the process. In time the women state what they want to learn and the way they prefer to learn it, and they indicate the parameters of the process that best fit their needs. This recognition and articulation of what they need is often a big step for them, individually as well as collectively. One funder suggested that "the process used in Candora is where we all need to be."

But that process takes time and energy on the part of the women. When negotiating with a funder, the coordinator often takes four to eight women with her to the funder's office. The intention is to educate the women and to gain negotiating power from their numbers. The experience is also part of the process of their learning to take control of their lives. The former coordinator related how the women use funders' Christmas parties to accomplish some of their programming goals. The usual expectation is that the coordinator will attend these functions and make connections on a social basis. But since all the Candora women are involved in program planning, the organization sends a number of women to these parties (two van loads, according to the former coordinator). The women thank funders who have contributed to Candora and confront funders who have not yet contributed money to support the program. In a sense this can be called a networking, bargaining, or counteracting strategy: networking for the women, bargaining for money for the organization, and counteracting—going outside the funders' usual frame of reference—by sending a number of women to the parties. This strategy has two outcomes: for external purposes, it gains what the women want; and for internal purposes, it provides material for the women's dialogue at Candora.

Likewise, when Candora is asked to make a presentation, the whole group goes and sits in the first row. There is a sense of empowerment and ownership when the women do the talking for themselves. This is another instance of counteracting power. The assumptions are that one person cannot speak for the lived experiences of all and that many women are needed to relate to those in the audience who hold the power in society, in order for those people to understand and to learn. The coordinator often walks a fine line in these settings. Getting funding depends on the funder's agreeing with the program's objectives. If he or she is alienated by these displays of collectivity, the program's funding can be placed in jeopardy. In most instances, since going en masse is out of the ordinary and shows considerable effort on the part of the women, Candora obtains the funding. Alternative negotiating strategies are part of the philosophy of Candora, but they can be disturbing to the funder. The coordinator must read the context well to determine the best course of action.

Another dilemma for the coordinator concerns the use of instrumental tools as measures of progress, since collectives operate under a different paradigm. Candora is founded on the process and principles of dialogue and relationships, but last year one of the funders requested a type of program evaluation that did not capture these elements. Evaluation forms often require objective data and measures of goals met. This is difficult for Candora, as everyone is participating in a process—on a journey, so to speak—that is difficult to translate into statistics. The request for this kind of evaluation sparked critical reflection on the kinds of funds Candora would accept. The women asked such questions as, "What are the funders in it for? What are we doing this for? Whose purpose are we serving?" A sense of clarity emerged as these problems were addressed, and the women voiced their concerns to the funders. The women's intention is to always critically reflect on the language of funding agencies, to educate both themselves and the stakeholder. In the midst of conflicting interests, the Candora women use a bargaining strategy to explain how they operate. In the end, the funder that requested the objective evaluation could not be convinced to think a different way, and the coordinator did the evaluation using quantitative data. A decision was made on what was important; in this instance it was the integrity of the process of critical reflection.

The last example of a dilemma program planners may find themselves in concerns the preemployment funding that constitutes Candora's largest funding source. Candora's preemployment funding program is an expensive component of the overall program, because it runs for a full year at a time and pays its women to participate. They keep the number of participants low so that there will be ample opportunity for interaction in the group. When representatives from the government funding agency that provides Candora with preemployment funding visited the office, their emphasis was on obtaining quick-fix solutions to problems; they expected to see results in three months. Candora was willing to let go of the third of the program budget that paid the women, but they wanted to put something in to replace it, like an honorarium that would recognize the value of the changes the women had made in their lives and what they had given to each other and to Candora. The members of the collective felt that their commitment was worth something monetarily. They also wanted to keep the full-year program format, knowing that it takes time to make substantive changes in people's lives. However, Candora lost this preemployment funding program. This is another example of when the strategy of bargaining did not work. The women were not willing to compromise on the principle of paying women to participate in the program, and the consequences were high. However, they knew if they had accepted the three-month deal, they would have failed in honoring women.

Learning from Practice

The participatory model that Candora espouses is often difficult for people outside the organization to understand. The coordinator finds it hard to explain their methods to most government funding agencies because they are used to a certain way of doing business with the groups they assist. The coordinator feels very isolated at times and strives to seek out other practitioners who work in the same way. She must maintain her connections with existing and potential funders, however. There are risks in following alternative strategies. On the one hand, the coordinator must facilitate a process of planning that adheres to the principles of participation and equality. On the other hand, by giving voice to and demonstrating these principles, there is a risk that funders will feel threatened and withdraw their support.

The coordinator must work both within the normal avenues of program planning, such as networking, and outside them (assuming conflicting interests are present) to further the causes of the organization. This is the ethical dilemma that beleaguers program planners in grassroots organizations. They must be able to stand up for what they believe in and be willing to enter into conflictual relationships, but they cannot sacrifice the organization in the process. In institutional contexts, a program planner who stands up against the direction of her organization faces the possible consequence of losing her job. In the case of community-based organizations such as Candora, the consequence of standing up to funders may include losing the organization as well as the job. Unfortunately, this is becoming increasingly apparent in today's political climate, as funding is becoming much more conditional and programs more prescriptive. The balance of power has tilted toward the funders, and they are not willing to tolerate the generation of power on the part of learners. The rules of the game have changed dramatically, which makes it much more difficult for Candora.

In a changing political climate, political resources and relationships change. Information is contested, withheld, manipulated, and distorted. Now the problem is time—time to search for sympathetic resources, oppose the neoconservative agenda, and plan strategic action. Because the environment is composed of conflicting interests, incremental bargaining is the best strategy (Forester, 1989). Standing on principles is noble and ethically correct, but can Candora survive without acquiescing to political pressure for instrumental, technical, skilled-based programming? At what point do they compromise themselves and seek out funding that does not fit their needs, just so they can remain in existence? There is an ongoing tension between having an organization that honors women's experiences and needs and simply sustaining the organization. Sometimes the bargaining in the negotiation process is successful; other times it is not. Nevertheless, incremental bargaining often seems to be the best strategy to use.

Through the case study of the women in Candora, we have sought to contextualize community-based program planning. Analyzing the political climate, conflicting interests, and power relationships in grassroots organizations contributes to a more specific and complex understanding of emancipatory learning in program planning than the present literature provides. When these elements are identified by consensus, dialogue and critiques are essential to planning and acting appropriately. The aim is to uncover the premises or assumptions that guide actions and consequent policies. When rationality is at play, it is possible to use such strategies as networking, bargaining, and counteracting power for negotiation. However, we are not convinced that rationality is the key player in program planning, at least not with the women of Candora. Attempting to capture the complex nature of women at work collectively was a hard process, as angry feelings, doubts about personal worth, and courage to speak, for example, are often nested in nonrational conditions. Evidence for nonrationality existed throughout our research in the community. It existed when the women spoke about their lived experiences, and it was provoked when they went en masse to meetings, which is outside the experiences of funders and others in the middle class. Personal relationships are built around nonrational criteria rather than hard, political interests. Also, the attempt to justify a technical, rational approach to community-based programming is actually founded on nonrationality. Nevertheless, the coordinator must be aware of both the nonrational and rational aspects of negotiating for power. The effect of using an approach that provokes nonrationality, such as counteracting power, could be greater clarity regarding the interests of both community program planners and external stakeholders. While we argue for incremental bargaining as the best strategy based on this research, we also recommend that planners not fear the strategy of counteracting, for sometimes it is through conflict that our best learning occurs as a community.

We cannot end this chapter without acknowledging the complex subjectivities and the ethical standards of the women we interviewed for this project. We found the courage they exhibited in disclosing the conditions of their lives and the strength they possess to be great. In a country where the social net was at one time considered vital to a just and humane society, these women are beginning to fall through the cracks. While it might be easier to acquire funds by accepting funder guidelines, somewhere along the way someone has to ask, "Can what we propose actually be done under these restrictions?" There are always ethical dilemmas that emerge when one poses questions like this, and the consequences of such decisions are often hardest for those who are marginalized in society.

References

Candora. *We Are Candora: The Candora Story Written by the Women of Candora.* Unpublished manuscript, 1994.

Cervero, R. M., and Wilson, A. L. *Planning Responsibly for Adult Education: A Guide to Negotiating Power and Interests.* San Francisco: Jossey-Bass, 1994.

Clarke, C., Kilmurray, A., and Lovett, T. *Adult Education and Community Action.* London: Croom Helm, 1983.

Forester, J. *Planning in the Face of Power.* Berkeley: University of California Press, 1989.

Freire, P. *Pedagogy of the Oppressed.* (M. B. Ramos, trans.). New York: Continuum, 1970.

Hamilton, E., and Cunningham, P. "Community-Based Adult Education." In S. B. Merriam and P. Cunningham (eds.), *Handbook of Adult and Continuing Education.* San Francisco: Jossey-Bass, 1989.

Hart, M. "Thematization of Power, the Search for Common Interests and Self-Reflection: Towards a Comprehensive Concept of Emancipatory Education." *International Journal of Lifelong Education,* 1985, *4,* 119–134.

Hart, M. "Liberation Through Consciousness Raising." In J. Mezirow and Associates, *Fostering Critical Reflection in Adulthood: A Guide to Transformative and Emancipatory Learning*. San Francisco: Jossey-Bass, 1990.

Heaney, T., and Horton, A. "Reflective Engagement for Social Change." In J. Mezirow and Associates, *Fostering Critical Reflection in Adulthood: A Guide to Transformative and Emancipatory Learning*. San Francisco: Jossey-Bass, 1990.

Lovett, T. *Adult Education, Community Development and the Working Class*. Nottingham, England: University of Nottingham, 1982.

Lovett, T. (ed.). *Radical Approaches to Adult Education: A Reader*. London: Routledge, 1988.

Thompson, J. "Adult Education and the Women's Movement." In T. Lovett (ed.), *Radical Approaches to Adult Education: A Reader*. London: Routledge, 1988.

SUE M. SCOTT is associate professor in adult and higher education at the University of Alberta in Edmonton, Canada.

MARGO SCHMITT-BOSHNICK is completing her master's of education degree in adult and higher education at the University of Alberta. She has worked in community education and postsecondary education for the past twelve years.

Cervero and Wilson provide a new set of optics for understanding planning. Their framework challenges long-held views of what's important and is a useful, though imperfect, tool for improving practice.

Negotiating Power and Interests in Planning: A Critical Perspective

Thomas J. Sork

The Hubble space telescope was launched with great fanfare in 1990 because it promised images of unprecedented clarity that would reveal the secrets of distant galaxies. By aiming the telescope and its sophisticated instruments at long-observed but little-understood celestial formations, humans would learn a great deal about the origins, characteristics, and dynamics of the universe. As the world learned shortly after the Hubble was in orbit, flawed optics initially rendered it useless for its most important tasks. Astronomers using the telescope at the time could not be certain whether dots on the images produced were important new discoveries or "artifacts introduced into the picture by the imperfect optics of the telescope" (Reston, 1995, p. 93).

Cervero and Wilson (1994) have provided adult and continuing educators with a new set of optics for viewing the complexities of program planning. Their framework would have us discard the technical-rational lens through which we have viewed planning for nearly five decades and replace it with a lens that brings into focus the social dynamics, or "people work," of planning. They argue that flaws in the technical-rational lens have seriously distorted our understanding of planning and that the lens of social dynamics promises to render a clearer picture of the essential character of the process. In their 1994 book they present three case studies of program planning to illustrate how focusing on social dynamics reveals significant new understandings that are missed when other lenses are used. Mills, Cervero, Langone, and Wilson (1995) also employ the social processes lens to study the dynamics of planning in a state's cooperative extension service. Their analysis concentrates on the relationship between the interests of planning actors and the outcomes and processes of planning.

The authors of the preceding chapters have used the optics supplied by Cervero and Wilson to view distinctly different cases of program planning with the intent of developing new ways of understanding and engaging in practice. My task is to be a critic of both the Cervero-Wilson framework and its application to the cases. I should be regarded as a friendly critic, because I have found the framework to be a very useful alternative to conventional ways of understanding planning. Although the optics they supply for viewing program planning in adult and continuing education are different in some fundamental ways from what existed before, the social processes lens has, in recent years, been increasingly applied to many aspects of educational practice. Their work represents an overdue application of that perspective to program planning. Part of the job of any critic is to warn of imperfections in the optics that may produce artifacts in our images of planning that could be mistaken for important discoveries. The case studies reveal some possible imperfections that will be discussed below, but first, a few issues about the framework itself need attention.

The Foreground as Contested Space

The foreground is always a limited and contested space. Cervero and Wilson have asked us to look at program planning in a way that places the power and interests of planning actors in the foreground. They argue that for too long the foreground of planning theory has been occupied by a concern with technique. By focusing on technique, important social, political, and ethical dimensions of planning have either been ignored or relegated to the background. Because it is impossible for either theorists or planners to give equal attention to all potentially relevant factors, what occupies the foreground tends to have an important influence on both theory and practice. What occupies the foreground in planning practice is determined by individuals, but what they place in the foreground is influenced by the ideas of others and their own experience. If placing the social dynamics of planning in the foreground is a greater help to planners than focusing on technique, then technique will be relegated to the background.

As the contest for the foreground continues, it is of great interest to consider the theoretical and practical implications of what ends up in this important space. It is also quite easy to fall into an intellectual trap by regarding the competing ideas as mutually exclusive and therefore incompatible occupants of the foreground. Cervero and Wilson do not fall into this trap, but they sometimes come close. In the sections that follow, I identify strengths and weaknesses of their framework as a way to think about and engage in planning. Whenever possible, I illustrate these points with examples from their book or from the chapters in this volume.

Negotiation as a Metaphor for Planning

In Chapter One, Wilson and Cervero clearly state their position regarding planning: "We argue that planners' work is always carried out in contexts that are marked by power relationships that will enable or constrain responsible planning. Because people's interests are causally related to the kinds of educational programs that are constructed, negotiation is the characteristic activity of program planning practice. The central responsibility of planners' practice, then, is to work out whose interests will be represented in the planning process."

Metaphors are powerful linguistic tools because they allow us to think about a phenomenon in new, creative, and more useful ways. Planning-as-negotiation-of-interests is a useful metaphor because, as the case studies illustrate, so much of the time spent in planning programs can be regarded as "negotiating among the actors." But however useful, the uncritical adoption of this or any other metaphor can result in a form of tunnel vision that blinds us to important aspects of the phenomenon that are removed from the center of the field of view. When the Hubble telescope is aimed at important objects in space, it does not record other objects or events that are out of its field of view. Even objects and events within the telescope's field of view might be missed by its sophisticated instruments if the instruments are not designed to "see" those objects and events. In other words, it is indeed useful to regard planning as negotiation, but we need to understand the dangers of only seeing "negotiations" when we look at planning practice. While focusing our gaze on negotiations among the actors, we may miss events and decisions that are not strictly tied to negotiations but that have an important impact on the program. A good illustration of this is found in one of the three cases described by Cervero and Wilson (1994). While planning a new program for a new audience, a fundamental but common error was made by the planning actors: they seriously overestimated the proportion of those in the "target group" who would likely register for the program. Being unaware of or not applying rules of thumb known to many planners and found in standard texts on promoting programs was one important factor that led to cancellation of the program. Responsible planning, then, is much more than negotiating; it also involves applying knowledge and skills that have only an indirect or marginal relationship to the power and interests of the actors.

Contained in the case studies are many examples of negotiation among actors, but little attention is given to the character of the negotiations themselves. Cervero and Wilson point out that planners not only act within the context, but also act upon the context. The analysis contained in the cases might benefit from the application of two theoretical frameworks used by Elgström and Riis (1992) to understand the curriculum revision process in Sweden. Their study used a combination of frame factor theory and negotiation theory to characterize the process that led to a significant change in the school curriculum. Frame factors refer to "such factors that constrain the intellectual space and the space for action within a process, which the actors at each point of time during the process cannot influence or perceive they cannot influence in the short run" (p. 104). Frame factors are important in understanding the social dynamics of planning because how they are perceived by planning actors determines the way they shape and constrain negotiations.

In my own practice, I tend to spend a great deal of time thinking about and discussing frame factors, often when others simply want to get on with planning. I suspect that this tendency is a function of experience and represents being too sensitive to the politics of planning. I have had many successful experiences in program planning and attribute some of them to being aware of frame factors and taking them into account early in planning. Some of my unsuccessful experiences in planning were in part attributable to not being aware of frame factors or believing that they were negotiable when they were not. But I also have a tendency to see frame factors where none exist and to sometimes believe I cannot influence a situation when I actually can. I am not sure if being aware of these tendencies makes me a better planner or just a more frustrated one, but I have recently found myself holding back my views on frame factors to avoid introducing constraints on planning where none may exist. The danger of holding back in this way is that planning may proceed without the actors' recognizing material constraints that should be taken into account, and this may result in delays when the constraints are confronted or in financial, political, or other problems when planning a subsequent program.

Cervero and Wilson's discussion of negotiation is rather general and is based on a critical theory of planning presented by Forester (1989, 1993). They focus on interests and power as key factors in explaining the social dynamics of planning, yet they do not distinguish between different kinds of negotiations and the role of interests and power in each. Elgström and Riis distinguish between two types of negotiations: substantive and meta. Substantive negotiations "take place under the umbrella of existing frame factors" (p. 105), while metanegotiations take place around these frames. As they explain: "In any decision-making process, some frame factors are by all actors perceived as given and impossible to change. Others are, at least by some actors, considered to be negotiable. One important type of potential frames in this respect are decisions specifying the decision-making *theatre, arena, actors, problems and solutions*" (p. 105, italics in original).

Metanegotiations involve reaching decisions about these matters: "By engaging in meta-negotiations, actors make attempts to change power relations and to reach a more favourable negotiatory position in re-opened substantive negotiations" (p. 105). The cases in this volume describe both types of negotiations, but no attempt is made to distinguish between them or to analyze the different strategies used in each. A deeper understanding of planning and a richer range of ideas about how to effectively engage in planning could result if a more complete set of analytical tools were provided that capture the complexity of negotiations.

Multiple Purposes and Planning

The case studies in this volume represent a fascinating assortment of explicit, implicit, and (occasionally) contradictory interests, aims, and purposes. For example, two explicit purposes of the health promotion coalition described in Chapter Three were the empowerment of residents and the reduction of risk factors for premature loss of life. On the surface these two purposes seem compatible and complementary, but as the case study reveals, collaborative planning involving diverse stakeholders provides a site where conflict occurs over which purposes are to be regarded as primary and whose interests will receive greater attention. Although Carter concludes that the steps of the empowerment planning model were followed, she warns that "it is very likely that planning, in particular empowerment planning, will get lost or subverted in the complex interplay of power relationships, interests, and sociostructural and economic factors in such environments." A small number of people occupy the limited space around the planning table, and it is these people who are able to influence decisions and promote their interests. The case aptly illustrates that "who is empowered" is largely determined by who has access to the planning table and who influences the decisions made there. It remains unclear whether the other purpose of planning—reducing risk factors—was achieved, because little energy was devoted to designing an evaluation plan to assess impact. Planning is always constrained by time, so the task of adequately addressing multiple purposes is an ongoing challenge. As real or imagined deadlines approach, those who are negotiating plans tend to focus on what they regard as primary purposes; purposes not considered primary receive less attention.

Another case that illustrates the challenge of multiple purposes is found in Chapter Five, in which Roger Maclean recounts the planning of continuing medical education (CME) programs in a university-based medical center. In this case, there were three purposes: an explicit and presumably "public" purpose, to help medical practitioners keep up-to-date with new developments in their areas of practice; an implicit and "private" purpose, to maintain or increase the number of cases referred to the medical center from primary care providers; and another implicit purpose, to maintain a high enough flow of income to the CME unit so it could maintain itself. As Maclean points out, "[an] evolving need that these programs serve is to increase referrals from primary care physicians so that the clinical practice increases, specialists are kept working, beds are full, and operating rooms are busy."

The interest of some stakeholders in maintaining or increasing referrals to the medical center was in partial conflict with the purpose of maintaining income flow to the CME unit because of pressure to keep registration fees low in order to attract the maximum number of primary care physicians. The pressure to generate income is well known to those in many continuing education operations and had the same effect in the case study as it has had in many other institutions. In at least one program area, allied health professionals and physicians located far from the medical center became marginalized client groups because they were not primary sources of referral income for the center. Those making decisions about programs were in a position to marginalize these client groups and did so to further the center's financial interests rather than the interests of health professionals or the general public.

Another complicating factor in this case was the presence of a total quality management program in the medical center and the related discourse centered around "customer satisfaction." Only by redefining *customer* could the CME unit claim progress toward higher satisfaction, because those being marginalized would certainly not be satisfied with fewer opportunities to attend relevant programs. Although this case and others in this sourcebook illustrate situations in which multiple purposes have influenced the planning process, we have learned more about the power of institutional interests than about how planners can use resistance and advocacy as negotiating strategies to further the interests of adult learners, who are often represented around the planning table by "proxy planners" (Rosenblum, 1985).

Sources of Power in Planning

To fully understand planning, we must understand where power comes from and how it is distributed, redistributed, and exercised. The power relationships among the planning actors in the cases described in this sourcebook are highly varied and dynamic. Some of the cases describe negotiations in which those who control access to resources were much more powerful than those seeking access to resources—and yet the interests of those in power were best served by making those resources available. In other cases a deliberate strategy to redistribute power was followed, with some success, to influence decisions in ways that were not in the best interests of those with the most power.

Several sources of power are evident in the cases. Some actors exercised power derived from their position as leaders with the authority to allocate certain resources. Others exercised power based on the number of people they represent and how active these people were in asserting their claims on resources. Other actors held power because they were able to work with others to pursue their interests if resistance or blocks were encountered. Some derived power from information they held and from their ability to withhold that information to further their own interests. It is even possible, as in the case described in Chapter Two by Barbara McDonald, to gain power by realizing that you are likely to lose your job regardless of the planning outcome. These are a few sources of power found in the case studies presented in this sourcebook.

Cervero and Wilson speak of the ethics of planning and suggest that an ethical stance must be taken on whose interests matter. Although they urge planners to act ethically, there is little discussion of how one justifies decisions to manipulate people and circumstances to pursue specific interests. There is little discussion of the moral justification for actions that could easily be viewed as manipulative or antidemocratic. McDonald rightly observed in her case study that "What has emerged so far from the planning process is a story of opposing personal and political wills and ideologies." Although she takes an ethical stance in favor of community activists, she misses an opportunity to present a compelling moral argument to justify that stance. If negotiating power and interests are the central features of program planning, then great care must be taken not only to recount details of the negotiations but also to reveal the moral and ethical justifications for actions taken. An ethically sensitive planning practice must not only acknowledge that an ethical issue was confronted but also be accountable for decisions made and actions taken in relation to the issue.

Actors and Their Identities

Several of the cases in this sourcebook provide detailed information about the characteristics of planning actors, while others provide little or none. When reading the cases that describe the actors in more detail, I began to wonder just what this information revealed that would help me understand why they acted as they did. For example, in the case in Chapter Three, we learn that one of the members of the health promotion coalition planning team is "an African-American family practitioner and division director within a large county hospital [who] has worked in several community health agencies and coalitions across the country and has contacts in the medical and academic community." In this brief passage we are given information on the actor's gender, race, social and economic status, education, current position, and networks. From this and other information provided we begin to form a mental picture of the actor and of his interests, influence, and power. With similar descriptions of other actors, we form images of these people and how they might engage with one another in the people work of planning. But how accurate and complete are these images, and to what extent are they based on stereotypes? Does having such information in case studies add depth to our understanding of the social dynamics of planning? Does it motivate us to more fully engage with the cases because we have images of the actors, or does it encourage us to reach facile and premature conclusions about planning? This and the case presented by McDonald in Chapter Two contain the most detailed information about the actors and contrast sharply with other cases that reveal little or no information about actors. If having detailed information about actors is important to our understanding of planning, then what contribution is made by cases that lack this information? These are rhetorical questions, because I don't have any answers. I did find myself drawn more fully into the cases that had more information about the actors, but I'm not sure why. I hope it is because these cases illustrate the complex interplay between the actors' identities, interests, and power, but it could be for the simple reason that these authors tell a more compelling story.

The issue of revealing the identities of planning actors in these cases has interesting implications for practice. As we engage in planning (that is, negotiate) with others, what information should we reveal about ourselves and seek to learn about other actors to strengthen our position as negotiators? Since we are trying to further our interests, it may be important to selectively reveal information about ourselves, lest we weaken our position. Being a middle-aged male of European heritage is difficult for me to conceal in any context; that I hold a faculty position in a respected university, teach in an adult education program, and grew up in the United States are typically revealed—directly or indirectly—early in conversations; that I grew up on a farm in California, was a Boy Scout and 4-H member, have a first degree in agriculture, am heterosexual, drew "lucky" number 318 in the Selective Service draft lottery of 1970, am a dual citizen of Canada and the United States, and voted "liberal" in the last federal election are rarely revealed, although they are arguably more relevant to the way I engage in planning. So I am left with many more questions than answers concerning the relationship between the identities of actors and how they engage in the people work of planning. It may be that we can make few predictions about how people will engage in planning based on what we know about them. The most important reason for learning some of the characteristics of planning actors may be that they provide a basis for establishing human relationships, acknowledging and respecting differences, and finding common ground on which programs can be constructed.

The Quest for Substantively Democratic Planning

Wilson and Cervero, in Chapter One and in their book, make a strong case for engaging in what they refer to as substantively democratic planning. They are unambiguous in their position: "The normative base for our theory rests on the belief that adult and continuing educators should actively promote a substantively democratic planning process." In taking this position, Cervero and Wilson are moving from the descriptive-analytic mode to the prescriptive. Quoting Apple (1992), they assert that substantively democratic planning means that "all people who are affected by a program should 'be involved in the deliberation of what is important.'" This position is certainly consistent with the growing expectation of many citizens that they will not only be consulted but that their interests will be taken into account when programs are planned and delivered. Several of the cases in this sourcebook likely meet this criterion of good planning, but it is very difficult to regard some of the planning reported here as substantively democratic.

In one respect, Cervero and Wilson's call for substantively democratic planning is nothing new; adult education planning theorists have been promoting the same idea using different words for more than twenty-five years. For example, Knowles (1970), in describing the andragogical process of program planning, emphasizes the importance of establishing a process for participative planning, and Boyle (1981) devotes three chapters to involving people in planning. The conventional wisdom that has permeated the literature is that responsible planners always involve those who have a stake in the program. Yet it does not take an elaborate research study to confirm that a good deal of program planning is neither substantively democratic nor occurs in a substantively democratic context. It is certainly true, as Cervero and Wilson point out, that countries like the United States and Canada have democratic traditions and institutions that invite citizen participation in making important decisions. Yet within these democratic contexts there are many examples where citizens do not accept the invitation to participate or are willing to have others engage in planning on their behalf.

One reason that substantively democratic planning is so rarely seen is that citizens have trusted others to represent their interests. However misguided, there are domains of action where citizens become involved in planning only when they sense a grievous violation of this trust. Many routine planning activities—including those in the domain of adult and continuing education—are carried out in less than democratic circumstances because those affected are happy to let others represent their interests. The call for substantively democratic planning is safe and politically correct, but as is the case for any universal prescription, we may reasonably ask if it fits all circumstances. The cases in Cervero and Wilson's 1994 book are clearly not examples of substantively democratic planning, yet they are good illustrations of everyday planning in which reasonable, well-meaning, yet fallible people work together to arrive at designs for worthwhile programs. If one of the purposes of adult and continuing education is to always promote participation and empowerment and to increase the sense of ownership that learners feel toward programs, then substantively democratic planning seems like a defensible, universal prescription. But to assert that all good planning should be substantively democratic seems too easy. A critical approach must challenge such a universal assertion and ask such questions as, "Under what circumstances is it important to ensure substantively democratic planning?" and "What are the consequences of not engaging in substantively democratic planning in this particular circumstance?"

Closing Remarks

I began this chapter by making reference to the Hubble space telescope and its potential to reveal important features of the universe that have been hidden from view. The Cervero-Wilson framework on program planning presents the same potential—and risks—for adult and continuing educators that the Hubble presents to astronomers. It provides a sharply focused image of an often-observed but little-understood phenomenon. Its analytical instruments are not as sophisticated as they might be, but they reveal features of the complex process we call program planning that were only fuzzy blotches when studied without the aid of these new optics. They have positioned us above the contaminated atmosphere so that we can get a better view of planning. Much work remains to be done to extend their analysis and to understand its implications for program planning, but their work represents a turning point in theorizing about program planning. We may not agree with their analysis, but we cannot ignore it. The cases presented in this sourcebook provide ample evidence that the optics they supplied reveal new and exciting features of the terrain of program planning.

Cervero and Wilson are fond of paraphrasing Forester (1989) by asserting that theories don't plan programs, people do. I agree that theories don't plan programs, but I suggest that people with theories do. This sourcebook challenges program planners to reconsider their personal planning theories and to consider adopting a more useful way of understanding and engaging in planning. When we are comfortable with our theories, we are reluctant to change them to account for new observations. But just as astronomers are being forced to reconsider their theories based on images from the Hubble, we must now face the task of changing our theories of planning to account for the central role of negotiating power and interests.

References

Apple, M. W. "The Text and Cultural Politics." *Educational Researcher,* 1992, *21* (7), 4–11, 19.

Boyle, P. G. *Planning Better Programs.* New York: McGraw-Hill, 1981.

Cervero, R. M., and Wilson, A. L. *Planning Responsibly for Adult Education: A Guide to Negotiating Power and Interests.* San Francisco: Jossey-Bass, 1994.

Elgström, O., and Riis, U. "Framed Negotiations and Negotiated Frames." *Scandinavian Journal of Educational Research,* 1992, *36* (2), 99–120.

Forester, J. *Planning in the Face of Power.* Berkeley: University of California Press, 1989.

Forester, J. *Critical Theory, Public Policy and Planning Practice: Toward a Critical Pragmatism.* Albany: State University of New York Press, 1993.

Knowles, M. S. *The Modern Practice of Adult Education: Andragogy Versus Pedagogy.* New York: Association Press, 1970.

Mills, D. P., Jr., Cervero, R. M., Langone, C., and Wilson, A. L. "The Impact of Interests, Power Relationships, and Organizational Structure on Program Planning Practice: A Case Study." *Adult Education Quarterly,* 1995, *46* (1), 1–16.

Reston, J., Jr. "Orion: Where Stars Are Born." *National Geographic,* 1995, *188* (6), 90–101.

Rosenblum, S. H. "The Adult's Role in Educational Planning." In S. H. Rosenblum (ed.), *Involving Adults in the Educational Process.* New Directions for Continuing Education, no. 26. San Francisco: Jossey-Bass, 1985.

THOMAS J. SORK is associate professor of adult education in the Department of Educational Studies at the University of British Columbia.

Planning responsibly requires educators to learn to read situations in terms of power relations and interests.

Learning from Practice: Learning to See What Matters in Program Planning

Arthur L. Wilson, Ronald M. Cervero

That Thomas Sork would choose to draw an analogy between our work and the Hubble telescope is more than a bit prophetic, for our central point in this chapter is that responsible planning is a matter of learning to see what matters. As Sork suggests in Chapter Eight, what planners see depends entirely on how they "foreground" their activity. His last point, that people plan programs *with* theories of what needs to be done and how to get it done, is precisely what we and Forester (1989) have argued. To be sure, planning work is people work, as the cases presented in this sourcebook demonstrate. But understanding people work depends on which theories we use to see it. Traditionally, we have used the logic of planning steps to see planning work, and that view brings very important aspects to the foreground of practice. We do not, however, believe that our concern with power and interests replaces our technical responsibilities as planners, as Sork suggests. Rather, we must see those traditional planning tasks—as these cases amply illustrate—as centrally involved in who has the power to represent which interests. Thus, the instrumental tasks of conducting needs surveys, establishing objectives, selecting content and instructors, designing formats, administering programs, and evaluating outcomes are important, because they tell planners what to do and also because they are the activities within which planners negotiate power and interests. So their significance lies not just in their technical execution but in the political and ethical consequences of whose interests come to the foreground of planning and whose interests are downplayed. Learning to see, then, is a matter of seeing these political dimensions of planning so that our practice can be more responsible.

NEW DIRECTIONS FOR ADULT AND CONTINUING EDUCATION, no. 69, Spring 1996 © Jossey-Bass Publishers

Our purpose in this chapter is to suggest some recommendations for practice, drawing upon the cases presented in this sourcebook and on Sork's insightful critique to discuss three ideas. First, we draw attention to the idea that planning requires a way of seeing and that responsible planning requires a particular way of seeing. Second, we suggest that learning to see is part of learning how to read planning situations. Third, we synthesize some insights from the case studies about what really matters when planners see the world of planning practice from the perspective of negotiating power and interests.

Seeing Our Responsibility for the World We Make

Why does planning matter? As planners, we construct educational programs that change the way people think and act. By acting in the world to somehow make it different, planners use their power to negotiate interests to directly produce the concrete features of educational programs. Which programs get constructed are a direct result of whose interests dominate the planning. This is why we continually say that because the actual form and content of educational programs depend upon the interests of those who construct them, the central responsibility of planners is to determine whose interests they will negotiate in the planning process. So it really matters whose interests are represented in the planning process. With this ethical responsibility in the foreground, planners can begin to see how the "people work"—that is, the politics—affects their planning and how they represent interests.

Because interests always matter, responsible planning requires a particular way of seeing. Foremost among planners' concerns should be to put real choices before the representatives of all those involved in or affected by planning, which is what we mean by engaging in "substantively democratic" planning. Sork raises several good points about this ethical premise. His primary suggestion is that such a principle is not well developed and should not be a universal prescription. We agree that it clearly needs to be better developed; our intent here is to promote more discussion. We believe this conversation has just begun. Sork is right to say that somewhat similar calls have characterized the literature for years. Indeed, the link between adult education and democratic principles is a prominent feature of adult education discussions. He is also correct to say that substantive democratic processes are rarely seen in planning practice; he argues that this is so because "citizens have trusted others to represent their interests" because they are "happy to let others" do that. This leads Sork to say that for us "to assert that all good planning should be substantively democratic seems too easy" because it is "safe and politically correct." We must, however, disagree with Sork's explanation of why planning is rarely substantively democratic.

While we, too, are ambivalent about universal precepts, the substitution of technical competency for moral clarity leads rapidly to relativistic planning, in which those with the most power make the decisions. In general, this is the classical problem with technical rationality (Forester, 1989). This is precisely what happens when adult learners "trust" professional adult educators to make their decisions for them. For example, with the exception of the Candora program in Chapter Seven, every case in this sourcebook represents adult educators' constructing educational programs with little or no substantive involvement of the learners (although the planners often carefully involved other interested constituencies, such as institutional leaders and teachers). This is an issue of power—who has the means to say and implement what matters—not a matter of convenience, efficiency, or professional competency. It is exactly this issue that characterizes the planning literature. Yes, the literature promotes learner and stakeholder involvement in the planning process and charges planners with some obligation to promote such involvement. But the problem with the democratic calls that Sork refers to is that they are defined procedurally, not politically. Thus, when learners are put in circles and asked what they want to learn or when stakeholders are brought together in meetings to decide others' fates, without a clear ethical mandate to act politically in promoting substantive involvement, the dominant power relations are reproduced and ensure that the interests of the more powerful will control the construction of the program. Such a planning process, while appearing participatory, is hardly democratic in practice or consequence.

Substantively democratic planning is not a procedural task, as it is routinely promoted, but an ethical stance requiring the execution of political strategies. Such a stance often requires fundamentally altering power relationships, which is surely not what the planning literature means when discussing learner and stakeholder involvement. We have pointed out earlier (Cervero and Wilson, 1994) that a significant outcome of planning is the maintenance or transformation of planners' power to construct programs. Furthermore, planners typically know this and actively seek to either maintain or strengthen their ability to act. In every case presented in this sourcebook, whether or not it involved democratic planning, the planners acted to change power relationships. Even in the seemingly "everyday" examples of the distance education programs described by Kleiber in Chapter Six and the Nursing Achievement Program described by Hendricks in Chapter Four, the planners explicitly acted to change relations of power in order to construct certain kinds of programs. Our point, however, is that without a principle of involvement by which planners are willing to act politically and challenge who has the power to say or do what matters (such as in the CityGreen and Candora cases)—especially when those interests and powers run counter to the substantive involvement of others, as they often do—planning practice will continue to reproduce dominant power relationships, whether they are in the best interests of learners, teachers, planners, institutional leadership, and the affected public or not. Worse, by defaulting to the traditional ethic of the field—by which educators are seen as experts in means, not ends—planners become by allegiance and in their activities the representatives of the dominant interests in any specific planning situation. Thus, we disagree with Sork's suggestion that professional competency by itself warrants paying less attention to the crucial ethical concern of negotiating interests in every planning situation.

It is extremely important, however, for planners to respond to Sork's questions: when is it important to ensure substantively democratic planning, and what are the consequences of not doing so? Our agenda is less to formalize a universal prescription than to raise a question that must be considered in every planning situation. Sork is right in his assertion that the case studies in this sourcebook miss several opportunities to elaborate upon the ethical justifications for planners' actions, for each of the practice examples represent important choices about whose interests really matter. Even so, the cases demonstrate succinctly how significant those justifications are to responsible practice. That the planners had difficulty in articulating their ethical justifications indicates how embedded those concerns are in their day-to-day practice and how difficult it is to extract them abstractly. For example, in McDonald's case study of the CityGreen Project, representation is clearly at stake in terms of whose interests will determine the form and content of the program. McDonald describes the difficult and dangerous *political* acts necessary to challenge dominant interests and power. Yet, an ethical justification for her explicit actions (such as persuading McKee to "speak for" her) is only suggested. As Sork asks, are McDonald's actions justifiably representative, or are they the result of a political contest between two powerful planners with different interests? Likewise, in the Scott and Schmitt-Boshnick case, representation is a key issue, and the planners develop clear political strategies (such as group visitation of funders' offices) to alter the power relationship between the Candora women and the other stakeholders. Is this justifiable, particularly given Scott and Schmitt-Boshnick's concern that it might jeopardize the program? In Carter's health promotion case, it is ironic that the planners actively follow an empowerment procedure without the active involvement of the learners or the affected public, the usual starting place for empowerment practice. Yet the political strategy of combining 501(c)(3) and grassroots groups actually results in providing access to resources that some community groups have traditionally been denied. Even so, does the top-down logic of "empowerment" in this case actually empower traditional groups, or does it extend the community's professional dependency? The other cases may be less substantively democratic, and perhaps, as Sork suggests, they do not need to be. Nonetheless, justifying the representative consequences of political strategies clearly is not easy, nor is it a matter of simply following a procedure. What the cases do consistently indicate, however, is how crucial the connection is between intent and strategy and why in every situation planners have to negotiate the issue of representation.

Because interests are causally related to which programs get constructed, our point is that responsible planning requires a particular way of seeing: responsible planners care about whose interests are represented, and they are willing to act politically to ensure their representation. Thus, we see the central activity of planning as deliberative, not authoritative—because planning is about outcomes, not just process as is typically supposed. What really matters in planning is which programs get constructed, not just the process of their construction. Placing the negotiation of power and interests in the foreground as the substance of the traditional tasks, and thus seeing their political importance, leads directly to understanding how the outcomes of planning are different depending on how we see things. Traditional planning manuals start with procedures and learners and tell planners how to process inputs. We believe this is rather myopic because, as these cases indicate, we do not just plan programs for adult learners. Sork suggests that there are other legitimate reasons for planning programs, and the case studies exemplify that point. We agree, which is why we ask whose interests count in the construction of programs. Without an ethical stance on what matters, the dominant interests and power relationships will determine which programs get constructed. This is why we use the image of learning to see—planners must attend to who is being included and who is excluded, because different programs will result. If McDonald had not seen who matters in the CityGreen project, the dean would have retained control and produced a program that served only his interests. If Kleiber had not seen how the information generated by surveys about her students was useful for negotiating access to campus departments, segments of a learning population would have gone underserved. In Maclean's CME case, if the planners had failed to see the relationship between referrals and continuing education, their program base and institutional support might have shrunk. If Hendricks chose not to develop a collaborative staff, the Nursing Achievement Program would have underserved its target population and may well have been discontinued for lack of achievement. Without exception, each case has illustrated how planners use political strategies—that is, how they manage the people work—to negotiate certain interests that produce specific programs. This brings us back to our starting point, which involves our claiming responsibility for the way the programs we plan change the way people think and act. Planning responsibly means actively accepting the risks and rewards of the outcomes of our planning work. Why is planning important? Because our planning process and the programs resulting from that process change the world, depending upon what we see and choose to respond to (or, in our lexicon, which interests we choose to negotiate). Thus, our way of seeing is fundamentally connected to what happens, not just how to get it done.

Learning to See Means Learning to Read Situations

Because being responsible requires a particular way of seeing, planners must learn to read the situations in which they work. If planners cannot, do not, or will not learn to read the often uneven, sometimes explicitly treacherous terrain of planning practice and instead opt to provide "technical assistance" (to the familiar cry of "I don't get involved in politics"), then as we said earlier, their work will tend to serve the most powerful. So what do planners have to do? First, as we have argued, planners must have an ethical framework that is concerned with more than just what works, and, we suggest, they should possess a representative one as well. Second, planners must be willing to act strategically (that is, politically) to promote their ethical interests (the case studies amply demonstrate planners' willingness to act politically). However, acting politically to be responsible requires planners to interpret (or, as Sork would say, "foreground") their understanding of planning arenas and activities in certain ways. The contest here is about which "theories" will best help planners to read their situation and thus help them act more responsibly. We have offered a particular set of analytical optics to help planners to see—power, interests, negotiation, and substantively democratic planning.

Planners have to be able to read the power and interests in a given planning situation; if they do not, they will not be able to tell whose interests are going to count and how to use their power to negotiate them. In turn, how planners read the situation—how they manage the people work, how they see the politics—affects which interests dominate and which get excluded. This means, of course, that different programs will get constructed.

Regardless of the difference made by the planners described in this sourcebook—each planner's actions produced substantive changes—all the planners demonstrated their ability to read which interests matter and to determine who has what power to get things done. In each case the planner's reading of the situation resulted in specific political strategies for negotiating interests and managing the people work of their planning. The political volatility of the City-Green Project is clear and probably represents to many planners their worst nightmare about getting involved in the politics of planning. Yet McDonald's reading of the power and interests led directly to her strategies for managing the politics of the situation. While some people may be uncomfortable with her strategies, it is clear that if she had not counteracted the dean's power, the implemented program would have violated the intended outcomes of the planning. In Carter's report on the health promotion program, the planners used their reading of the situation to develop an innovative funding strategy that got around traditional obstacles and allowed new grantees to secure resources. In the Nursing Achievement Program case, Hendricks's reading of the situation as fragmented in terms of location and uncollaborative working relationships led to her strategy of renegotiating the program location and involving all the staff in a mutual planning project. Whose interests matter and who has what power clearly result in different programs.

Likewise, there is no doubt that in Maclean's continuing medical education case significant programmatic opportunities would have been lost had the planners failed to read the situation in terms of how important the institution's interest in patient referrals was. As with Hendricks's case, Kleiber's distance education program has an "everydayness" in its seemingly lacking a contest of power and interests. Yet, if Kleiber had failed to use her student population information to challenge the perceptions of traditional academic departments or to use her division's programmatic policies to her advantage, then a significant population would have gone underserved. As in the CityGreen case, the

Candora case clearly represents a contest of interests and power. In this case, if the planners had opted for the traditional technical assistance role, then clearly the funders and government bureaucracy would have produced a very different program. Instead, the planners acted politically to represent their ethical interests to challenge the power relationships—and again, a different program was constructed. The point is that none of these planners acted as a technical expert in the planning process—the traditional role defined for the adult education planner. Rather, each planner's work represented a skilled reading of the power and interests involved and a skilled execution of political strategies to manage the people work of planning. Their strategies directly reflected how they read the situation. All these planners recognized their role as *political* actors with explicit ethical interests in producing not just the process of planning but its very outcomes. Central to these different outcomes was how the planners read their situations.

Learning from Practice: Learning What to See

It is quite possible to map traditional planning procedures onto one's planning practice. In fact, almost twenty years ago, when Pennington and Green (1976) first asked about what planners actually do in their practice, they were critical of planners who did not precisely follow the prescribed steps. This tradition is still well in force today. But in recent years, as we indicated in Chapter One, studies of planning practice have begun to reveal a different world of work than what the literature prescribes. Sandmann's comment (1993) bears repeating: as much as planners might like to think that they are following the steps of planning, much of their work has to do with managing the tensions of practice, or as we have described it, the people work. It is clear to us, as Sork notes, that traditionally the instrumental tasks of planning have taken a privileged place in the foreground of our understanding of what planners do. Our point is not to displace the importance or necessity of that work but to see it in a new way: the planning tasks are important for the political and ethical consequences of whose interests are negotiated in constructing educational programs. While negotiation is the characteristic activity of planners, in performing these tasks, power and interests are negotiated.

Although the literature continues to privilege the instrumental tasks, we suggest (and the case studies presented here demonstrate) that it is actually irrational to follow the same steps in every situation. Different circumstances call for different responses. For example, Kleiber's strategy of using student survey data to gain access to academic departments would fail to produce the same results for McDonald in negotiating with the dean. Similarly, the planners in the Candora case promoted the Candora women's taking responsibility for their program, a strategy that clearly would not work in Maclean's continuing medical education situation. And even though they share similar circumstances, the health promotion coalition's strategy of restructuring the grant process would not have made any sense for Hendricks's Nursing Achievement

Program. Our point is that planners need to learn to see with, as Sork says, a new set of optics. Quite simply, if planners do not learn to read the situation in terms of power and interests, then their technical skills become the instruments of the dominant interests in the planning situation. So without seeing how power and interests work in planning, planners will not be able to tell whose interests will prevail.

It is clear that in making these claims we are moving away from the rhetoric of an adult-learner focus, common in the literature, and more toward what we think is the reality of actual practice. By looking at and learning from practice, the central question becomes how planning practice serves and reproduces certain interests by validating whose knowledge counts. Educational practice always occurs in a culture of knowledge and power, and planning has to be seen as substantively contributing to the maintenance or alteration of who has the power to say and do what matters. Every single case demonstrates how power and interests matter in terms of which programs are constructed. So, yes, as Sork says, planners always plan with theories—in terms of how they think the world works, which directly produces the actions they take as planners. How planners read the situation, how they manage the people work, and whose interests they choose to represent demonstrate their theories of what matters and directly affects not just the process but the educational programs that planning produces. It is clear that different programs result, depending upon the ethical and political actions of the planners and the interests they represent in those political actions.

We believe that experienced planners know a lot about this way of seeing and routinely have practical conversations with one another about the people work of planning. So what does our point about learning how to see mean? Our response is that by making those practical conversations more public, we can better see how central responsible planning practice is to adult and continuing education. More specifically, we think that an understanding of the specific conditions of each planner's situation is crucial to responsible planning, which is why it is so important to see conditions defined as power and interests and responsibility defined as substantive representation. Even so, across the varied contexts described in this sourcebook—contexts ranging from expert-driven delivery systems (Maclean, Kleiber, and Hendricks) to programs devised by agents of the community (McDonald, Carter) to community-based collective empowerment programs (Scott and Schmitt-Boshnick)—there are several insights we can gain.

By way of closing, we offer these insights as a way of continuing to expand our way of seeing what really matters in planning educational programs for adults:

Planners must learn to negotiate power and interests responsibly, because their actions (that is, their planning tasks) validate whose interests matter.
Because power and interests matter, planners must learn how to anticipate sources of support and potential obstacles to plan responsibly.

In order to anticipate, planners must determine the power relationships by figuring out who counts and who should count.

Planners must know who they are responsible to (that is, whose interests matter, both politically and ethically).

Planners must learn to read their individual situations in these terms, because only by doing so will they be able to see their ethical and political choices more clearly.

References

Cervero, R. M., and Wilson, A. L. *Planning Responsibly for Adult Education: A Guide to Negotiating Power and Interests.* San Francisco: Jossey-Bass, 1994.

Forester, J. *Planning in the Face of Power.* Berkeley: University of California Press, 1989.

Pennington, F., and Green, J. "Comparative Analysis of Program Development in Six Professions." *Adult Education,* 1976, 27, 13–23.

Sandmann, L. R. "Why Programs Aren't Implemented as Planned." *Journal of Extension,* 1993, 31, 18–21.

ARTHUR L. WILSON *is assistant professor in the Department of Adult and Community College Education, North Carolina State University.*

RONALD M. CERVERO *is professor in the Department of Adult Education, University of Georgia.*

INDEX

ORDERING INFORMATION

NEW DIRECTIONS FOR ADULT AND CONTINUING EDUCATION is a series of paperback books that explores issues of common interest to instructors, administrators, counselors, and policy makers in a broad range of adult and continuing education settings—such as colleges and universities, extension programs, businesses, the military, prisons, libraries, and museums. Books in the series are published quarterly in Spring, Summer, Fall, and Winter and are available for purchase by subscription and individually.

SUBSCRIPTIONS for 1996 cost $50.00 for individuals (a savings of 34 percent over single-copy prices) and $72.00 for institutions, agencies, and libraries. Standing orders are accepted. New York residents, add local sales tax for subscriptions. (For subscriptions outside the United States, add $7.00 for shipping via surface mail or $25.00 for air mail. Orders *must be prepaid* in U.S. dollars by check drawn on a U.S. bank or charged to VISA, MasterCard, or American Express.)

SINGLE COPIES cost $19.00 plus shipping (see below) when payment accompanies order. California, New Jersey, New York, and Washington, D.C., residents, please include appropriate sales tax. Canadian residents, add GST and any local taxes. Billed orders will be charged shipping and handling. No billed shipments to post office boxes. (Orders from outside the United States *must be prepaid* in U.S. dollars by check drawn on a U.S. bank or charged to VISA, MasterCard, or American Express.)

SHIPPING (SINGLE COPIES ONLY): one issue, add $5.00; two issues, add $6.00; three issues, add $7.00; four to five issues, add $8.00; six to seven issues, add $9.00; eight or more issues, add $12.00.

DISCOUNTS FOR QUANTITY ORDERS are available. Please write to the address below for information.

ALL ORDERS must include either the name of an individual or an official purchase order number. Please submit your order as follows:
Subscriptions: specify series and year subscription is to begin
Single copies: include individual title code (such as ACE 59)

MAIL ALL ORDERS TO:
Jossey-Bass Publishers
350 Sansome Street
San Francisco, California 94104-1342

FOR SUBSCRIPTION SALES OUTSIDE OF THE UNITED STATES, contact any international subscription agency or Jossey-Bass directly.

OTHER TITLES AVAILABLE IN THE
NEW DIRECTIONS FOR ADULT AND CONTINUING EDUCATION SERIES
Ralph G. Brockett, Susan Imel, Editors-in-Chief
Alan B. Knox, Consulting Editor